Craft

Poems

Printed and published in Great Britain by D.C. Thomson & Co. Ltd., 185 Fleet Street, London EC4A 2HS. (c) D.C. Thomson & Co. Ltd., 2004

ISBN 0 85116 853 1

£5.99

TO BE A FARMER'S SON

by Joyce Stranger

Somehow, the lamb became a symbol of how good life could be — if only he could let go of the past . . .

WIND screamed across the fields. The mountains loomed black, their tops capped by snow.

"Your father's late, Ben," Rachel said, her voice rough with anxiety.

"He's not my father." It was an old argument, well-worn and exhausting, and his mother had no time for it now. Not with heavy snow forecast, and Gwyn away for too long, in the old and unreliable Land Rover.

"He's my husband." Anger sharpened her voice, and so did the sudden knowledge that she was ill. Pain throbbed behind her temples, and she couldn't bear even the thought of having to cook a meal.

"So?" Ben's shrug was more than she could bear. She'd thought that in the two years since she'd married Gwyn, Ben would have become reconciled to his stepfather.

It was six years since Pete had died. Six years since that fateful knock on the door, when his colleagues in the police force had told her how, in trying to arrest an armed robber, Pete had been shot.

Ben's father had been a hero, and no man could ever replace him in the boy's eyes. He seemed to think his mother was a traitor — that she should never have remarried. They'd been fine, the two of them, until this interloper had come into their lives.

She knew that was how Ben was thinking. He'd told her, too often, lashing her with words until she felt as if she could stand no more.

He'd been such a sweet little boy, when he was tiny.

Where did that child go, she wondered now, her eyes turning to the darkening windows, to the threatening clouds that hung like a heavy pall in the surly sky.

Ben rushed out of the house, and down to the bottom of the garden. There, he could close his eyes and pretend he was back home.

This wasn't home, this huddle of farm buildings under the hill.

Home was a warm house in a suburban street, with his friends just next door and his father returning from work, swinging him high in the air and saying, "How's my boy?" in his deep voice with the faint Somerset burr, so unlike the Welsh lilt of the man his mother had married on that dreadful day.

The farm was so far away from everything he had known — he couldn't even go to the churchyard to put flowers on his dad's grave. He couldn't go to talk to him . . .

Are you anywhere up there, he asked the stormy sky, and then shivered as he felt the first touch of snow.

The sheep were in the high field, but they would have to be brought down nearer the house. His stepfather would have moved them if he'd been here.

Where was his stepfather? Why hadn't he come home? Had there been an accident? For the first time worry pricked at Ben, too.

If his stepfather died, who would look after them? Who would look after the farm?

THE sky was darker now and the threatening storm was almost upon them. Ben went back into the house. His mother lay back on the old settee, her face white.

"Ben, I think I've got 'flu. I feel so ill. You'll have to cope . . . the sheep . . ."

She was shivering, her teeth chattering. Ben was terrified. Suppose his mother died? There would only be Ben and his stepfather then — and they hardly ever spoke to each other.

His stepfather had tried and eventually given up. Ben had refused to answer him, refused even to make any comment directed at the man he resented so much.

He fetched the duvet from his mother's bed. Then he filled a hot water bottle and made her a hot lemon drink, which she sipped, but could not swallow. He tried to ring the doctor, but the phone was dead.

And then he remembered the sheep . . .

He went out and released Mott, the big sheepdog. The dog had never worked for him, and he was half afraid of the big collie. "Bring the sheep down, lad," Ben said, trying to copy his stepfather's voice.

He opened the gate that led to the top field and Mott sped through on fleet legs, rounding up the herd, working without command, working as he knew he must work, bringing the sheep down to the safety of the field near the house, and finding any that were buried in the drifts piled against the hedges.

At last it was done and the dog lay, panting, watching Ben, who closed the gate. Every sheep was safe.

HE went into the barn for hay. He worked on, even when the snow came. The dog nudged his knee.

Time for food? Ben went into the kitchen and filled the stainless steel bowl with meat from a tin, but Mott ignored it and continued to bark and nudge at him.

Ben stared at him and then followed. The dog led the way to the far end of the field, where a ewe was struggling to give birth to her lamb.

What should he do? Ben raced indoors to find his stepfather's books about sheep. The lamb was the wrong way round, he knew, and with the phone lines down and the snow beating against the house, there was no chance of getting a vet.

The book was not helpful. What should he do? He ran back. The ewe was lying on the ground, all breath gone from her body. She was dead, but the lamb was alive.

A little ewe. He lifted her and took her into the kitchen.

The milk recipe was on the dresser, as his mother always made up the bottles for the orphan lambs every year.

He read it and weighed out the powder and boiled the kettle. He settled himself in the big armchair that belonged to his stepfather, the lamb on his knee. It was so small, and yet it struggled to live.

It breathed and twitched its tail and ears and as he held the warm milk to its mouth, it began to suck noisily, and the little tail wagged in a frenzy of delight.

The dog settled against him.

There was wonder in Ben's eyes. This little creature had been born only minutes before and yet it held on to life with such vigour.

The ewe had died, but the baby survived and went on living.

"Let me go, son," his father's voice seemed to say. "What matters is what lies ahead."

The words were so vivid that he almost expected to see his father before him.

Outside, the sound of an engine choked and died, and his stepfather came into the room, shaking snow from his feet. He stared at his stepson.

Ben stared back, aware of his immense relief, and the startling knowledge that he was delighted to see Gwyn home at last.

"The ewe died," he explained, "but I managed to save the lamb. It's feeding well."

"That was well done. Was it the big ewe with the torn ear?"

Ben nodded.

"She shouldn't have been in lamb at all — she was far too old. You did well, son. The lamb's yours, if you want her. Start of your own flock, like?"

"I'd like her," Ben said. Then, "Mother's ill," he added, suddenly remembering. "I tried to get the doctor, but the line's down."

In an instant, Gwyn had crossed the room to Rachel, and was kneeling at his wife's side, touching her forehead, asking how she was, his concern evident.

"Looks like 'flu," his stepfather said eventually, his voice reassuring. "There's a lot of it about — lasts three days or so. She'll be right in no time. We can look after her, can't we?"

"Sure," Ben said, and was rewarded by his mother's smile.

THE days passed and the snow turned to slush. Ben and his stepfather worked side by side, carting hay, sorting out the lambs and marking each mother and lamb with the same number.

Ben's was special, the only lamb unmarked. He fed her by hand until she was old enough to go out to grass with the others.

He walked up the field with her in his arms, reluctant to let her go. He wondered if she would remember him.

He sat down on a bank, holding the little sheep close, knowing that she had changed his life.

The farmhouse that had seemed so alien, was suddenly home.

He held the lamb, and as he did so, said goodbye to the boy he had been. He had to grow up, so that both his fathers could feel pride in him.

He looked up at the sky.

"I won't forget you, Dad — not ever," he said. "But it's time to move on."

He held the lamb for a few minutes longer, feeling comforted, knowing she belonged to him.

She was the future, and one day he would be a farmer, like his stepfather, and make this farm one of the best in the county.

There was a whistle from the house. Ben put the lamb down on the ground, and ran back across the fields, revelling in the unexpected sunshine.

His stepfather was waiting for him at the door.

"Your mother's proud of you, lad," he said gently. "And so am I."

Words wouldn't come — not the right words. Ben felt tongue-tied, and then remembered his ideas for the future.

"Will you show me how to train a dog? Can I have a pup?" he asked.

His stepfather smiled, and opened the kitchen door. There, on the rug, sat a fat sheepdog puppy, his eyes full of wonder as he stared at the boy.

Ben ran to him and picked him up, and held him.

As he looked into his stepfather's eyes, he knew that they understood one another. In that moment he felt that he had everything in the world that any boy could want.

That night, when he went to bed, he thought that his father's face looked approving. He stood there in his uniform, looking out of the photograph.

Ben cuddled down to dream of a future in which he and his dog won every trophy that a sheepdog could win, and the world was filled with clapping hands.

He woke with the sound still in his ears, and went to the window.

There, at the edge of the field, a small ewe lamb was looking towards the farmhouse, waiting for him to come to greet her. ■

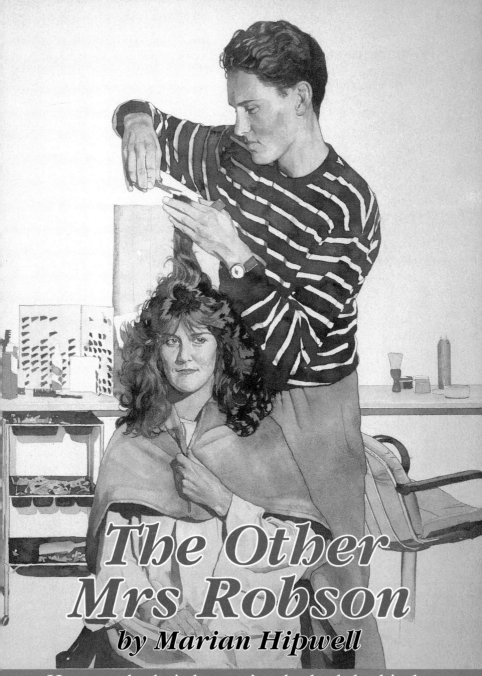

The Other Mrs Robson

by *Marian Hipwell*

Here, at the hairdresser's, she had the kind
of encounter every second wife dreads...

PUSHING open the door, Angela hurried inside the hairdressing salon. She was early for her appointment, yet with the rain beginning to fall outside, she didn't want to linger in the street.

"Mrs Robson?" The hairdresser's assistant smiled at Angela as she closed the door behind her. "Won't keep you long."

"That's all right, I know I'm early," Angela assured her. Taking off her coat, she settled down to wait. She'd been coming here for some weeks now; it was inexpensive, and the staff were friendly.

She'd always had unruly hair, and now, with the baby on the way, she'd been finding it difficult to manage it at all. Whoever said your skin and hair improve with pregnancy hasn't met me, she thought ruefully.

The salon door opened again and a woman, some years Angela's senior, entered the shop. Glancing up idly, Angela's smile froze.

It was her. Jim's first wife. She recognised her immediately. Not that they'd ever met, but she'd seen some old family photographs which Jim had shown her.

True, the other woman was older now, but Angela had no doubt it was her. She sat down to wait, favouring Angela with a brief smile.

With an effort, Angela forced herself to remain calm. What did it matter, anyway, if this woman was Jim's first wife? She'd never had any reason to feel guilty; he and Mary had separated before she ever met Jim.

They'd grown apart over the years, Jim had told her when she'd asked about the divorce; in fact, it had been Mary who'd suggested they should separate.

What a coincidence, Angela thought now, for them to meet like this! Was Mary a regular customer, or was it a trick of fate which had brought them both here on this cold Spring morning?

Whatever, there was nothing she could do now but bluff it out and make her escape as quickly as possible. At least the other woman didn't know who she was.

"You can sit here now, Mrs Robson." Angela held her breath as the hairdresser called her over to the sink. If the other woman was going to put two and two together, it would surely be now . . .

Yet there was no response, no quick turning of the head, no sudden realisation in the eyes of the woman sitting next to her. Instead, she'd picked up a magazine and was rifling idly through the pages.

TRY as she might, Angela couldn't relax as the assistant helped her into a gown and began to shampoo her hair. She was hardly aware of the water running over her head; all her thoughts were concentrated on the woman sitting by the window.

The moment she sat up from the sink, her gaze spirited in that direction. The other woman was watching her with interest, and Angela quickly looked away.

Did she know? Had she guessed? Yet Robson was a common enough name. There was no reason to suppose the other Mrs Robson was aware of her identity.

Not that it mattered, she told herself again. But it did, it did. All she wanted was to get this over with as quickly as possible and leave the shop, run back to her own secure little world where this other woman had no place.

Yet another part of her was glad that this had happened; glad to have the opportunity to put flesh to the ghost of the first wife.

She looked a little tired, she thought. Not glamorous or elegant as she'd sometimes imagined her to be; nor did she look forbidding and bitter.

The assistant showed Angela to a chair at the front of the salon, and the hairdresser began to trim her still-damp hair, chatting casually. Angela, unable to relax, glanced across again at Jim's ex-wife.

The other woman was being ushered across to the sink, where she slipped her arms into the sleeve of the gown offered to her.

Angela willed the hairdresser to hurry up, so that she could be moved to the hair-drier. Once underneath, the noise of the drier would drown out any attempt at conversation the other woman might feel constrained to make.

She could barely hide her relief when the hairdresser told her he'd finished, and the assistant motioned for her to move to the bank of driers.

She was soon joined by the other Mrs Robson, who sat down in the chair next to hers. Not long now, Angela thought. With luck, her hair would be dried and she would be out of the shop before the other woman came out from the drier.

Yet it felt strange to be seated beside the woman who'd shared so many years of Jim's life. There were so many things she'd have liked to ask about him — what he'd been like when he was young; how he'd been with the children when they were babies.

It seemed odd to think they had so much in common, herself and this woman, and yet so little. There was a barrier between them which neither could cross, even if they'd wanted to.

The first wife and the second wife could never really become friends, even if the divorce happened long before the second wife came on the scene.

"WHAT dreadful weather we're having at the moment." Angela jumped as the other woman turned and spoke to her. The hair-driers were noisy, but the other woman seemed determined to chat.

"Yes, it's been so wet lately." It would have been churlish of Angela not to have responded, yet she felt unable to talk naturally to the other woman. Opening a magazine, she concentrated on it.

"Your hair's a lovely colour." The other woman spoke tentatively. "Would you be annoyed if I asked if it was natural?"

"Of course not. Yes, it is naturally auburn," Angela replied. Praying that the older woman would drop the conversation, she returned to her magazine.

"Cup of tea, Mrs Robson?" the hairdresser offered, looking at the other woman. Angela had already refused a drink when he'd asked her.

She held her breath as her companion accepted the offer. Should she remark on the coincidence of their having the same name, she wondered? And if she did, where would that lead?

Her heart sank as the other woman began to chat again. To her relief, the topics of conversation were impersonal.

They exchanged pleasantries about the new shopping centre, and about the best place to get a cup of coffee. The other woman even told her of a shop she didn't know about, where she could buy lovely baby things.

"I noticed you were pregnant," the other woman explained. She hesitated, then went on, "It's lovely when you're expecting your first. I've got three, but they're older now, of course."

Angela looked down. She knew all about Sam, Clare and the eldest, Karen; she'd met them several times, in fact.

They were pleasant children, and friendly, once they'd overcome their initial awkwardness at meeting the woman their father had married.

They were the sort of children she'd expect Jim to have. Yes, and this woman, too.

Because whatever she'd imagined her to be like, the reality was different. She looked a nice person, the sort Angela would have liked as a friend, in other circumstances.

And, despite everything, she was glad they'd met. She was no self-assured, beautiful woman, this first wife of Jim's, but an ordinary human being for whom some things had gone wrong.

And, from what Jim had said, she'd recently met someone, a fellow student at evening classes, who shared her interests in a way Jim had never felt able to do.

Angela felt warmed suddenly. She was glad for this woman, glad she'd found herself someone to love. Glad, too, that they'd met in this strange way, rather than meeting as the two wives of one man, with all that that would entail.

There would have been no choice then but each to stay firmly on her own side of the demarcation line, the past warily confronting the present.

Thank heavens the other woman hadn't realised the truth . . .

HER hair was dried quickly and she was soon back in the hairdresser's chair. She was aware of the other woman's eyes on her as her hair was brushed out, and reassured herself that it was only a woman's interest in watching another woman's hair being styled. She did that herself, didn't she?

Even so, she was glad to pay and leave the shop. At the door she turned, unable to help herself. The other Mrs Robson's eyes were on her and, as Angela caught her gaze, she smiled and raised a hand in farewell.

"Hope all goes well with the baby," she said.

"Thanks. 'Bye."

Despite the still blustery weather, Angela was glad to be out in the open air and putting some distance between herself and the shop.

She'd never go there again, she knew. Yet, in spite of everything, she didn't regret going there this particular morning.

From under the drier, the other woman watched the pretty auburn-haired figure walk away. Thank heavens the girl hadn't realised . . .

It had been no accident, the two of them coming into the salon on this particular morning. A chance remark from the hairdresser when she'd booked her appointment had alerted her last week, coupled with the fact that she knew Jim and his new wife lived in this area.

She still hadn't been sure until she'd walked in and seen the girl her children had described to her in such detail.

Her eyes were thoughtful as the assistant brought her back to the hairdresser's chair. Second wives weren't the only ones who had ghosts to lay.

She'd been plagued for a while now by the thought of the younger woman her ex-husband had married, even though her own life with Jim was over.

Yet, far from being the glamorous redhead of her imaginings, the new Mrs Robson was just an ordinary young woman, the sort she'd have been glad to have as a friend. One day, perhaps.

But for now, it was best that they remained just passing strangers . . .■

Past Her Best

by Della Galton

My husband wanted to trade in our old banger for a younger, sleeker model. My fear was that he felt the same about me!

S HE'S going and that's final." Paul's face softened when he saw my bleak expression. "Look, I'm sorry, Jean, but keeping her just isn't practical any more."

The trouble was, I knew he was right. Unreliable, rusty and long past her best, Ethel might have been a classic car, but she just couldn't compete with the sleek modern versions being churned out of the factories in their millions today.

Not that we could afford a brand-new car — Paul's seven-year-old, ex-company car was the closest we came to that — but most cars on the road were at least ten years younger than our ancient Morris Traveller..

"I used to have one of those," was a common cry as I stopped at the newsagent's or outside the supermarket.

"Best car I ever had," and, "Go on forever, don't they!" were other remarks, usually accompanied by fond expressions and invariably from people emerging from sleek modern cars.

But I didn't see Ethel's rust — instead I saw an old friend who'd been with us through thick and thin for the past 15 years. I didn't mind her shabby interior as Paul did.

I was more inclined to remember the children as toddlers, clambering around on the grey leather, and hear the echoes of ancient picnics when she chugged faithfully into the forest on Sunday afternoons.

"We'll get something nifty and economical instead," Paul said, and started to clear away the tea things with a conciliatory expression on his face.

"A hatchback maybe; it'll be much easier for getting the shopping in and out — and it won't be past its 'sell by' date," he added, trying to make light of the situation.

I nodded grudgingly, but didn't smile. I knew I should be glad that he was concerned about me, but I just couldn't bear the thought of parting with her.

Call me sentimental if you like, but a lot of our past was tied up in Ethel.

It seemed ungrateful, callous even, to consign her to the scrap heap now.

"Perhaps we could advertise her in the classic car section in The Echo," I suggested to Paul, as I helped him carry the plates through to the kitchen.

"Mmmm, I think the 'under three hundred pounds' column might be more appropriate," he began, and then, seeing my expression, "OK, we'll give it a go. I don't want to see the car scrapped any more than you do, love."

LATER, we watched television in uneasy silence. Even the children were quieter than normal. The rock music which usually blared out of Andrew's bedroom was muted, and Laila had evidently decided the atmosphere at the pictures was preferable to staying in.

"The advert will go in on Friday," I told Paul, "so hopefully we'll get some interest over the weekend."

I knew my expression contradicted my words, but he just smiled brightly and said, "Great, that'll give us plenty of time to look around for a new model for you."

That night, as I undressed for bed, I studied myself critically in the mirror. I was past my "sell by" date, too, I thought, as I studied my thickening waistline and grey hair. What did Paul see when he looked at me? Did he notice the changes the years had brought in me as he noticed the deterioration in Ethel?

I frowned at my reflection. Don't be silly, I told myself. There's a world of difference between a person and a car.

But even so, the thought niggled as I curled beneath the sheets half drowsing, and listened to the familiar sound of Paul moving about downstairs.

I tried to be cheerful over the next few days because it seemed so silly to sulk. After all, if I'd insisted, I knew Paul would have let me keep Ethel, albeit reluctantly. But I also knew that the mounting repair bills and increasing difficulty he had in getting parts would make my insistence seem very selfish.

And on Friday, to both my and Paul's obvious surprise, we were inundated with phone calls about our "classic car".

A steady stream of people turned up from four o'clock onwards to look at Ethel, some with an eye to acquiring a cheap car, but some with a view to restoring her to her original glory.

There was one man in particular, an oldish fellow with ruddy cheeks and bright blue eyes, who was obviously an enthusiast.

"Don't make them like this any more," he murmured, running his hands lovingly over the old paintwork. "Won't see any of the rubbish they made today still on the road after twenty-five years."

"She's always served us very well. I'm reluctant to let her go," I told him, ignoring Paul's raised eyebrows and slight frown.

"She'll have a good home, I promise you that," the man told me. "I used to have one of these cars when the police used them, years ago, and I've wanted another ever since." His eyes misted over as he stared into his past and Paul and I exchanged glances.

"If it makes you feel any happier, I'll bring her round to let you see her when she's fully restored," he promised. "She'll look lovely with a bit of work."

Paul held my hand as we watched him drive proudly away.

"Well, you couldn't want for a better home for her, could you?" he commented, when they were finally out of sight.

"No," I agreed.

"So you're happier now?"

I nodded, but I don't think he was any more convinced than I was as we walked back inside.

THE smart white hatchback that we bought the next day didn't seem to improve matters either. Everything about it felt strange and awkward.

"You'll get used to it," Paul said confidently. "You've got to move with the times, love. You can't live in yesterday."

But somehow his words unnerved more than reassured me, and again I wondered how he saw me these days. Was he content with this older, cuddlier version of me, or did he long for the slim 20-year-old of our early days — or worse?

Paul wasn't the type to hanker after a younger woman, I told myself, as I bought a home hair dye kit in the supermarket and a book on diets.

He didn't comment on the darker colour of my hair, and merely raised an eyebrow when I served up baked potatoes instead of the usual chips for the third night running. He did, however, remark on the new black sequined top he spotted hanging on the wardrobe door.

"When are you planning to wear this, love?"

"The New Year's Eve dinner dance," I replied. I could feel a blush creeping over my face.

"Are you sure it'll — er — fit you?" he said dubiously.

"It will when I've dieted into it." My voice sounded a lot more confident than I felt, and then suddenly, and for no apparent reason, I burst into tears.

"Darling, whatever's wrong?" He was across the room in an instant. "Is it something I said? What is it?"

And then it all came pouring out, about Ethel and the memories tied up in her that I'd treasured so much, and finally all my fears that he might be wanting a younger model wife, too.

He didn't interrupt at all, and when at last I'd ground to a halt he still didn't say anything, although the arm he'd put round my shoulders at the start of the deluge stayed firmly where it was.

Then, to my confusion and surprise, he stood up, strolled over to the mirror on the wardrobe door and began to undo the buttons on his shirt, one by one.

"Do you remember our wedding night?" He reached the last button and patted the curve of his stomach ruefully. "I didn't have this then, did I? Or these."

He bent his head close to the mirror and pointed at the silver hair on his head, the silvery moustache, and then again at the framework of tiny wrinkles round his eyes. "Or these."

He came back across the room and sat down on the bed beside me.

"What I'm trying to tell you, my love, is that we can't expect to look like spring chickens any more, but we're growing older together, and we have a wealth of memories that we share." He smiled then, a smile full of warmth and gentleness.

"I know that Ethel meant a lot to you, but this way you won't have to watch her deteriorate for the lack of care that she'll get in a professional's hands." He paused long enough for me to snuggle into the reassuring curve of his arms.

"Am I making any sense at all?"

I nodded. Somehow everything was starting to make more sense than it had for a while.

"Perhaps I was just feeling a little insecure," I murmured into the familiar scent of Paul's hair. "Perhaps it's about time I went in for an MOT."

Tenderly he drew my face round to his and kissed my forehead. "In my book, love," he said softly, "you'll pass every time . . . " ■

HOME

A poem by
Joyce Stranger,
inspired by
an illustration
by Mark Viney

To me
Sterility
Is a house
Which is a showplace
Where rich folk live.
Where no-one plays or laughs
Or indulges in the kind of conversation
That is relaxing.
No small creatures
Frolic in the perfect rooms.
No one calls.
They are afraid of leaving footprints,
Rumpling the rugs
Or crumpling the cushions.
Nothing is shared.
I don't call that living.

To me
Fulfilment
Is a house
Where children romp and riot and laugh.
Where the cat has her kittens in the kitchen.
Where the dogs have their own places in each room.
Where in spring there are lambs in the barns to feed from bottles.
Where for the rest of the year ewes wander beside a boulder strewn
stream,
Where by day birds sing and at night owls cry.
Where even in winter when trees are bare
The sky is blue with massing clouds.
The distant hills are alive with colour.
The fields are green.
I pause from my work and sit on the wall.
I see smoke lifting from the chimney.
When I go in nothing will be tidy.
The dogs will race to greet me,
The children come to meet me,
And shout, "Dad's come home."
My wife will smile and put food upon the table.
And I know that I am rich.
I call that living.

The Intruder

by A.E. Groom

**Oh, she was kind enough and blonde and
pretty — but she was still coming between
Paul and his dad . . .**

IT was Friday, the best day of the week for Paul. The day Dad got off work early and came to meet him from school.

Paul's mum had died four years earlier when he was five and ever since there'd just been the two of them. But they were great pals. On Fridays they always went to McDonald's for tea and planned how they were going to spend the weekend.

Rushing through the school gate, Paul saw that his dad's car was there as usual. But he was puzzled because someone else was sitting in the passenger seat. Someone else was sitting in his seat in the front!

As Paul climbed into the back, he noticed that the car seemed to have a different smell — a sweet, flowery one. He supposed it must be because of the person sitting next to Dad. A lady.

"Thelma and I work together," his father explained, and then, "Thelma, this is my son, Paul."

"Hi, Paul!" the woman said, turning round and smiling.

Paul noticed she was blonde and pretty.

"Hi," he mumbled.

He supposed his dad must be giving Thelma a lift somewhere. He hoped it wasn't far.

He was dying to talk to him about the railway book he'd been reading at school that morning. And to ask him if they could go to ride on a steam train one day. Perhaps even this weekend.

But Dad didn't drop Thelma off anywhere. He parked in the car park behind the burger place as usual and then said, "I thought it would be nice if Thelma had tea with us tonight, Paul."

Nice! Paul couldn't think why it would be nice at all. Thelma probably didn't like beefburgers anyway. Most likely she lived on salads, like his Auntie Valerie did. He frowned as they walked through to the restaurant.

Inside, Dad said he'd fetch the food . . . "while you and Thelma get to know each other."

Get to know each other. Paul scowled. Why would they want to do that?

Thelma smiled again and they took their seats at a table by the window. "Your dad told me you like coming here, Paul," she began.

What a stupid thing to say.

"Yeah, it's all right," he mumbled, as he kicked the leg of the table and looked down at the floor.

"Don't you ever get tired of beefburgers?"

"No."

Thelma gave up at this point. And Paul stared at the floor until his dad came back with the food.

During the meal, Thelma asked him about his favourite football team, and offered to treat him to a special ice-cream afterwards.

But he said no thank you to the ice-cream, and he wouldn't talk. All he wanted was to have his dad to himself, to laugh with him over their private joke about beetle-burgers and French flies. And to tell him about his day at school.

Still, not long now, he thought as they piled into the car. Not long until we're on our own again.

So Paul just couldn't believe it when Dad said, "How about coming back with us for a coffee, Thelma?"

He clenched his fists.

How could Dad do that! How could he?

Don't come, don't come, he prayed silently in the back of the car.

"Thanks, David," Thelma said regretfully, "but I can't manage tonight, I'm afraid. Some other time perhaps."

Thank goodness! Paul almost sighed with relief and smiled for the first time that evening.

But there was no stopping Dad.

"How about Sunday then? Like to come to the coast with us, Thelma?" he asked. Her face lit up.

"Oh, that would be nice! I'd love to come."

"Great!" Dad was really chirpy. "See you Sunday, then, won't we, Paul? I'll give you a ring in the morning."

Paul pretended he'd dropped something on the floor. There was a tight angry feeling inside him that he couldn't explain. And he couldn't answer his dad, he just couldn't.

At last they dropped Thelma off at some flats and drove on home.

But the evening had been too spoiled to put right.

Even when they were inside, Dad seemed different. Far away somehow, and so Paul put on the television and didn't tell him about the lovely train book.

SUNDAY was a beautiful sunny September day. And if Paul and his dad could have just been left to build a whopping big sandcastle, or play cricket on the beach, Paul knew it would have been a perfectly happy one.

But there was Thelma, putting shells and silly flags on the castle. And dropping the ball all the time in cricket. She couldn't bat to save herself either, so that Paul was almost glad when the day was over and they went home.

And things didn't get any better.

After that there were many more weekends spent together. Followed by lots of evenings when the lady next door came to sit with Paul while his dad took Thelma out for a meal or to the cinema. And his father seemed so happy, as though something marvellous had happened to him.

And then one evening at the beginning of November, Dad broke the news.

"My firm want me to go up to Edinburgh for a couple of weeks, Paul . . ."

Paul looked up and big blob of paint dropped off his brush on to his colouring book.

"Edinburgh. Ooh! Can I come, too?"

"No, son — sorry. I'll be staying in a hotel and there would be no-one to look after you while I was working. And you'd have to miss school, too."

Paul made a face and wiped off the blob and started painting again, just so that Dad didn't guess that he was worried.

It was on these sorts of occasions that Paul could see how nice it would be to have a mum. But he pushed that thought to one side.

"Anyway," Dad went on, "you'll be all right, Paul, because Thelma's offered to come and stay here while I'm away. She'll make your meals in the evenings and get you off to school in the morning. Isn't that kind of her?"

Kind! Paul's fists were clenched again. Didn't Dad realise he didn't want Thelma around? He bit his lip and felt for one awful minute he was going to cry. But then Dad was speaking again.

"Otherwise," he was saying, "you'll have to go and stay with Auntie Valerie, Paul, and —"

Auntie Valerie! Oh, no! Paul remembered the last time he'd gone there on his own. Porridge for breakfast, salad for tea.

"Take your shoes off, Paul. Have you washed your hands, Paul? Now you don't want that silly old TV programme on, do you, Paul?"

It wasn't that he didn't like his aunt, but he just couldn't bear the thought of staying there.

It really looked as if he had no option. At least Thelma liked chips.

Dad was obviously pleased when he settled for Thelma, and when she came round the following Saturday, he spent ages showing her where everything was in the kitchen and telling her about picking Paul up from the child-minder's on her way home from the office.

"Don't worry about us, David," she said brightly. "We'll be fine, won't we, Paul?"

Paul just nodded. He couldn't muster any more enthusiasm. He really didn't think they were going to manage very well at all.

Saying goodbye to his dad the following Sunday afternoon was quite hard. His father put his arms round him and hugged him and told him to be a good boy and he'd speak to him on the phone.

Then he smiled at Thelma and hugged her, too, before he got into his car and drove off with a cheery wave.

"Now," Thelma said, looking a bit pink as she shut the door, "what shall we do?"

She seemed to say that quite often in the next few days, and Paul hadn't a clue what to answer. He and his dad often played Scrabble or draughts, or even noughts and crosses.

He was sure Thelma wouldn't know

about any of those and so he was quite surprised when, on the third night of her stay, after tea (he had to admit the meals hadn't been bad) she produced Monopoly.

"It's my favourite game from when I was young," she explained. "My nephew, Ben, likes to play it when he comes to stay."

Paul hadn't played Monopoly before, but grudgingly agreed. Against his will, he became very involved. The big piles of money, the little rows of houses and hotels, the fun of getting richer, going in and coming out of jail, and buying and selling property, was all so exciting. He was so wound up, he didn't want to go to bed.

"Tell you what," Thelma suggested, "we'll leave the board just as it is and carry on where we left off tomorrow night, shall we?"

"Oh, please!"

For the first time since knowing her, he really smiled properly at her. She smiled back broadly.

"Hurry up then and have your bath, Paul. Your dad was telling me you have a book about trains that you like. I thought we could look at that together before you go to sleep. My dad used to work for the railways so I know quite a lot about trains."

Later, as he drifted off to sleep, Paul's heart felt lighter than it had for ages.

HE really enjoyed the next evening, too. He and Thelma finished off the game of Monopoly, and he won. His dad phoned. And when Thelma put him to bed she showed him a book she'd brought with lots of pictures of steam engines.

At this rate the two weeks wouldn't pass too slowly, Paul thought — especially as Thelma said she could get off early on Friday and meet him from school like Dad did, and that they'd go to McDonald's.

As it happened, Paul's best friend, Michael, was there, too, with his mother. So they all sat together and the two ladies chatted.

The weekend was quite good fun, too. Thelma took Paul swimming on Saturday, and on Sunday they went to a country park and had Coke and buns in the café.

When they got back, Paul produced all his train books and Thelma seemed really keen and interested to look at them with him.

Everything was fine until Paul went back to school on Monday morning and was engrossed in feeding the gerbils when Michael came and stood beside him.

"I like your new mum," he remarked with much enthusiasm.

"New mum!" Paul dropped in enough food to keep the gerbils feasting for a week.

"What d'you mean, Michael?" His voice sounded odd. "That Thelma. She's nice, isn't she? My mum reckons she might soon be your new mum."

Thoughtfully, Paul replaced the tin of gerbil food in the cupboard.

It had been all right having Thelma around while Dad was away — much better than he had expected in fact — but to think she might be there for good! He wasn't at all sure about that.

He was distant and quiet when Thelma picked him up from the child-minder.

"What do you fancy for tea tonight, Paul?" she asked him brightly.

"Not bothered," he said shortly.

She went to take his hand as they crossed the road, but he pulled away from her. When they got indoors, he went straight up to his room.

Over tea (she'd cooked shiny brown sausages) she asked him, "Anything on telly tonight, Paul, or are we Scrabbling or money-making?"

He shrugged and pushed his plate away. There were five chips still on it.

"Paul," Thelma said, "are you all right? You're not sickening for something are you?"

"No, I'm OK."

Thelma looked worried. "Tell me what's wrong, Paul," she pleaded. "I thought we'd become good friends in the past week or so . . ."

Tell her! How could he tell her? He sat feeling uncomfortable, biting his lip, looking down at the table.

"I know," Thelma said softly at last, "you're missing your dad, Paul . . . Is that it?"

Paul squirmed and felt miserable, but before he could answer, she went on, "Well, he'll be back soon, Paul, and then we'll all be together and —"

But that wasn't what he wanted, was it?

"Not all," he burst out, "not all! Just me and Dad, me and Dad on our own, like we used to be."

They stared at each other for a minute, and then Paul turned and ran out of the room and up to his bedroom.

HE felt awful. Thelma had looked so miserable when he'd said that, almost as though she were going to cry. He didn't want to make her cry. He honestly didn't.

She was nice really. In fact, he didn't understand himself at all.

Then he heard her come upstairs. She put her head round the door and was obviously just about to say something, when the phone rang. Thelma went into his father's room to answer it, and Paul heard her say, "I'll take this downstairs, David." It was Dad then!

For ages, Paul stood there in the darkening room, listening to Thelma's voice in the hall below, but not hearing what she was saying.

Suddenly he couldn't stand it any longer.

He rushed into his dad's bedroom and carefully picked up the discarded receiver. He knew it was wrong to listen, but he couldn't help himself, somehow.

"Well, I suppose it's only natural, Thelma," Dad was saying. "Paul and I have been on our own for quite a while now, remember . . ."

"I know. I understand that," Thelma said, "and the last thing in the world I'd want would be to come between you. I'm too fond of you both . . . you know that . . ."

"I know that, love. Try not to worry. The important thing is, we love each other and we love Paul — that's all that really matters, isn't it? I'm sure it'll all work out . . ."

Putting the phone down quietly, Paul crept back to his room.

It all sounded so simple. Perhaps it was simple. After all, he did quite like Thelma now . . . Her voice interrupted his thoughts as she called up to him.

"Paul, your dad's on the phone. You can take it in his bedroom if you like."

Paul went back to his dad's room and lifted the earpiece.

"Hello, old son. Are you all right?"

Paul's voice quivered. "Y-Yes, Dad. I think so."

"Think so? What do you mean? What's wrong?"

Suddenly it all poured out.

"Well, I . . . I was horrid to Thelma just now, Dad . . . I didn't mean to be. I like her really, but —" His voice broke in a sob.

"Perhaps none of us is sure about anything yet, Paul — except that we all like each other very much. That's enough to be going on with, isn't it? We'll wait till I get home and talk about it then, shall we?"

Paul sniffed loudly.

"Yeah, OK, Dad. 'Bye."

He put the phone down. Then he heard footsteps, and quickly he rubbed his eyes. When he turned, he saw Thelma was in the room, smiling at him.

"I'm sorry, Thelma," he said, shyly. He was full of remorse for hurting her. And he knew that he'd be really sorry if she went away.

"That's all right, Paul." She smiled ruefully. "I didn't think you really meant it."

She held her arms out to him, and, without hesitating, he ran into them.

And she hugged him. And he felt warm and secure and happy again.

And then, as they went back downstairs together, another thought occurred to him.

"Thelma," he said, "do you like gerbils?" ■

"I Don't Want To Lose You..."

by Teresa Ashby

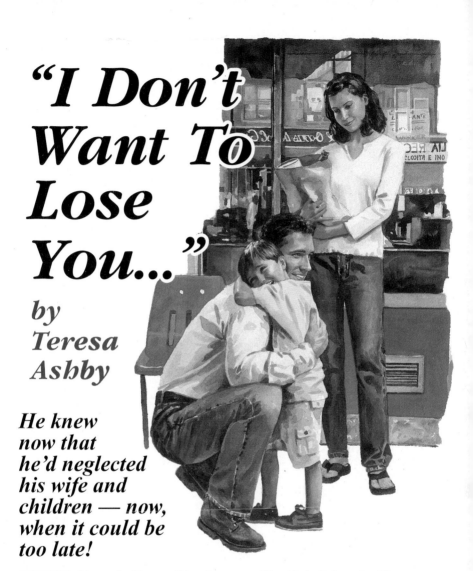

He knew now that he'd neglected his wife and children — now, when it could be too late!

THE old man had been talking for ages, telling Ned all those familiar tales of his past. He was a self-made man, who'd managed to escape the hardship and confines of the small northern town in which he'd grown up. These days he was a senior partner in a thriving law practice.

Ned smiled, nodding every now and then. He'd heard it all so many times before — about how success had nothing to do with luck, and everything to do with hard work.

"You've never had to work really hard to get anything," Harold Derby was saying to Ned. "You've had it easy."

Ned stared at him. Just because his parents had been able to afford to give him a good education didn't mean he'd had it easy! Money could buy privileges, but it brought pressures, too.

Ned worked for the firm of solicitors where Harold Derby was a senior partner. Harold liked nothing better than to regale junior partners, like Ned, with his own personal success story. Fortunately, the lecture also included a meal in the best restaurant in town.

It was, Ned often reflected, all part of the job.

His mind wandering, Ned scanned the restaurant, idly taking in the other diners.

He suddenly heard laughter he recognised. It was a very distinctive laugh, light and sparkling as champagne bubbles in a glass.

That's strange, he thought. Meryl didn't mention that she was lunching out today . . .

He strained to look across the crowded room, seeing Meryl a few tables in front.

He recognised the earrings she was wearing; he knew the soft curve of her neck, and the clinging shape of her dress.

As he stared, he caught the eye of the man sitting opposite her. He'd been laughing along with her. He was, Ned noted, good-looking, with dark eyes and a mouth crinkled with laughter.

He felt gutted. There was no other word for it. His wife here, with another man, laughing like that! When was the last time he'd heard her sound so happy, so carefree?

Tears unexpectedly stabbed his eyes. He didn't know what to do. Should he march up to their table and confront them? But what if he did that and she told him she loved this other man? Where would that leave him?

"If more people had to work hard to achieve things, then they'd appreciate them more. These days, too much is taken for granted . . ." Harold Derby went on, but Ned hardly heard the words.

She had been quite quiet lately, he realised. He'd automatically put it down to the children, never thinking he was to blame.

He'd seen the pain in her eyes sometimes, when she'd tried to talk to him and he'd said he was tired, too tired to listen. And he'd ignored her pain, pushed it away to the back of his mind, because he was just too tired.

"People have stopped caring," the old man was saying. "There's too much emphasis on the self these days, not enough thought given to the feelings of others."

When had Meryl stopped asking him to take them out at weekends? She always used to come up with suggestions for outings, but lately there had been nothing.

"I'm bushed," he'd told her, the last time she'd suggested a family day out. "I just want to stay at home. I don't feel like being cooped up in the car for hours on end. Besides, we should be saving up for that holiday in Corfu."

Suddenly, faced with the scene in front of him, the holiday seemed a very long way away. He reached for his wine glass and held it to his lips, his hand shaking.

HE had to do something, Ned thought in panic. But what? Perhaps it was too late even now . . .

He'd taken Meryl for granted, he knew, making sure his plans went ahead smoothly and hardly considering what she'd like to do.

He'd been wrong to assume that she was content to stay at home all day with two small children . . .

What was he to do, he asked himself desperately. He couldn't just sit here and let his marriage fall apart. He thought back to this morning.

Jasmine and Keith had leapt into bed between him and Meryl, snuggling down under the covers and giggling with excitement.

And what had he done? He was ashamed, now, to remember how he'd thrown back the covers and got out of bed, annoyed to have been wakened so abruptly.

He'd looked back and seen the three of them sitting up in bed, three sad, hurt faces. Meryl with her hair still tousled from sleep, four-year-old Keith with his ready smile, and little Jasmine with her pale blonde locks only just really beginning to grow.

"Daddy cross." Jasmine had stated the obvious in typical eighteen-month-old fashion.

Ned had looked pleadingly at Meryl, expecting her to explain to Jasmine that Daddy was in a hurry, but Meryl had simply turned her face away.

How many women had he seen in his office, made miserable by uncaring husbands? How many men had sat opposite him, full of tearful regrets because they'd lost everything through their own selfish indifference? Did he want his marriage to be the same?

He had to show Meryl he cared! On impulse, he stood up, but the table she'd been at was empty and a waitress was clearing away the plates. He'd lost his chance to confront her.

"What's wrong with you, Ned?" Harold snorted. "I'm sure you haven't heard a word I've said. That's what I've been saying all along, young people just aren't interested in listening.

"You've had it too easy all your life, but one day, if you're not careful, you'll pay dearly for it."

"I'm sorry." Ned sat down again, his mind in turmoil. "I thought I saw someone I knew."

Weak. He was a weak fool. What if she was gone when he arrived home tonight? He closed his eyes and pictured empty wardrobes, the floor devoid of toys, the house abandoned.

FIRST thing that same afternoon, Ned had an appointment with a client who was filing for divorce.

"I've turned a blind eye to his affairs all these years," the woman said.

"But now this girl's expecting his baby. I can't very well ignore that, can I?"

Ned shook his head sympathetically. The things some people put up with to hold their marriages together! Some would ignore anything, because while they ignored it, they could convince themselves that it wasn't really happening.

He saw a succession of clients that afternoon and managed to shut his own troubles out until it was time to go home. Then he was seized by a fear so powerful he almost didn't want to go.

He bought flowers for Meryl, and sweets for the children, then set off in his car for home.

Meryl was in the kitchen, preparing dinner. She always insisted the children ate with them in the evenings.

Ned stood in the doorway, watching her. She'd tried so hard to make them a complete happy family, and she'd had precious little help from him, he acknowledged grimly.

He moved across to her and kissed the nape of her neck. As she turned, squealing with surprise, he produced the flowers from behind his back.

"They're gorgeous!" she cried. "What a lovely surprise!"

She was happier, he could tell — much happier. But it wasn't surprise at being given flowers that had put that shine in her eyes, it was something that had happened at lunchtime . . .

"What have I done to deserve this?" she asked.

"You've been patient when I didn't deserve it," he said. "They're a thank you. And a promise that I'll change."

"Why should you change?" She frowned. "What's wrong with you as you are?"

"I can change," he said, trying hard not to sound desperate.

Jasmine and Keith rushed in then, happy to see him as always.

He gathered them both into his arms and hugged them tightly.

"What's wrong, Ned?" Meryl asked anxiously. "Has something happened at work? Are you ill?"

"You see!" he cried suddenly. "I'm so awful that if I hug the children and bring you flowers, you immediately think something must be wrong!"

"It's not that," she said, her frown deepening. "What's happened?"

The children, bored with being hugged, wriggled out of Ned's grasp and ran back into the living-room.

"Nothing." Ned sniffed miserably.

"You don't give me flowers for nothing," Meryl said tartly. "You've been seeing someone else, haven't you?"

"Me? Of course not! I love you, Meryl — I wouldn't do that to you. I might be a lousy husband and father, I might take you all for granted, but I'd never cheat on you."

"I'll put these in water then," she said, but her eyes remained troubled.

"I thought we could go away this weekend," Ned suggested.

"I thought we were supposed to be saving for Corfu!" she retorted.

"We can afford a weekend away. Maybe go to the coast."

"Not this weekend, Ned," Meryl said apologetically. "I've already made arrangements."

His heart leapt into his throat and lodged there. What arrangements? he wanted to ask, but he was too afraid of her answer.

AFTER dinner, Ned put the children to bed and read them a bedtime story. He was pleasantly surprised at how much he enjoyed it.

Too often he'd sit down after dinner with his newspaper and stay buried behind it until Meryl appeared to announce wearily that the kids were asleep. Now, he realised what he'd been missing.

Meryl had made coffee when he finally came downstairs.

"Don't you want to read your paper?" she asked in surprise, as he sat down and smiled at her.

"I'd rather talk to you," he said.

"Oh." She lowered her eyes and he saw a guilty flush rise to her cheeks. He didn't want to accuse her of anything. He wanted, like his lady client of the afternoon, to ignore what was happening and just hope that things settled down on their own. He was too afraid of losing her to do anything else.

"What about?" she asked, adding softly, "As if I didn't know."

"Anything you like," he said brightly.

"Is this what the flowers were for?" she asked.

"I do love you and the kids, Meryl," he said.

"But?"

"There are no buts, I love you. The old man was giving me one of his lectures at lunch and for once I listened. A lot of what he said made sense.

"I've always taken things for granted — my education, my job, you, the kids. I'd never even considered that I could lose any of it until today."

YOU went out for lunch?" Her voice was barely louder than a whisper. "Where did you go?"

"The usual place." He turned away so she couldn't see his eyes.

"You saw me there," she said flatly.

"You were there?" He tried to look surprised, but it wasn't working. She was looking at him pityingly.

"You know I was there, Ned. That's why you bought me flowers, why you're trying so hard to be nice. Obviously you were hoping to make me change my mind.

"Ned," she said carefully. "Since I've had the children, haven't you found me dull?"

"Dull?" he echoed.

"Don't laugh at me, Ned."

There was no doubting her expression now. Her eyes were full of tears, and she looked vulnerable. There was so much pain that he felt it for her.

"I wasn't laughing at you," he said softly. "I was laughing at the thought of ever finding you dull!"

"I had a good job before Keith was born, you know," Meryl went on. "It felt strange at first, becoming a full-time parent."

"But we agreed that it would be best," he said. "You didn't want anyone else to bring up your babies."

"I still don't! But that's when we began to grow apart. It was almost as if we were leading separate lives. You had your work, I had the house — and each excluded the other.

"It seemed the more I tried to involve you in what was going on, the more you resented us. In the end, it was easier just to stop trying."

He remembered, then, the days before the children were born. Days when there was just the two of them, living their lives as they chose. And now, while she'd adjusted to parenthood, he hadn't.

He was still living in the past, he realised, and instead of welcoming their children into his life, he'd shut them out, unconsciously resenting them for spoiling the way things had been . . .

"I had to do something, Ned!" Meryl explained, rousing him from his thoughts. "I couldn't go on like that any more."

"I see."

"I tried to talk to you about it, but you never seemed to want to listen. In the end, I decided just to go ahead."

He nodded angrily.

"The man I was with at lunchtime — Judd Carter — do you know him?"

"No, I don't," he said coldly.

He could hear the anger building up in his voice. Not anger at her, but at men like Judd Carter, who preyed on vulnerable and unhappy women.

"I knew you'd mind," she said defensively. "That's why I didn't tell you before. I was going to talk to you about it at the weekend."

"You were going to tell me?" He was incredulous.

"Of course I was." She smiled sadly. "You'd have found out sooner or later, wouldn't you?

"Anyway, I knew I'd have to tell you, because I'm relying on you to look after the children this weekend."

"You're not taking them?"

He was torn between relief and panic. At least he hadn't lost the children, too.

"Of course not! It wouldn't be much fun for them, would it?"

He couldn't contain his anger now. How could she be so cheerful when she was talking about the end of their marriage?

I WON'T let you go!" he declared, slamming his fist down on the arm of the chair.

"What?" she demanded.

"I love you and I won't let you go!"

"But it's only for a few hours on Saturday," Meryl said. "I thought it would help us . . ."

"How can your having an affair help us?" he cried.

"I'm not having an affair with Judd!" she countered. "What do you take me for? He's running a small business from his flat and he's got into a mess with his accounts.

"His wife is as useless with figures as he is and they're employing me to sort it all out for them!

"It's just a Saturday job, a few hours for me to use my mind, and a little time for you to use to get to know your children properly."

Ned stared at her, speechless.

"I was frightened of losing you," she explained. "You seemed so far away all the time, I thought I must be boring you. A job seemed the ideal solution."

Suddenly, Ned leapt to his feet and made for the telephone. He grinned at her as he tapped out the number.

"You're tied up at the weekend, but there's still tomorrow and Friday, right?"

"But you've got work —"

He put his finger to his lips when the old man's gruff voice answered the phone.

"It's me, Ned," he said.

"Ned!"

"I want to take a couple of days off, tomorrow and Friday."

"Why? What's happened? Is something wrong?"

"Nothing's wrong. I just want to take my wife and kids away for a couple of days, that's all. I'm not due in court, so if you could get someone to see to my appointments —"

"Well, thank goodness for that!" the old man exclaimed. "It's about time you paid some attention to that family of yours! Take the time off and welcome to it, lad.

"Was it something I said at lunch?" the old man asked.

"Something like that." Ned grinned. "Thanks anyway, Dad."

"For what?"

"For everything you've ever given me that I've taken for granted. And sorry for being such an ungrateful son."

Ned hung up after the call and put his arms around Meryl, holding her close.

"Fancy thinking I was having an affair," she said softly. "And there was me thinking you'd found someone else!"

"We should talk more —"

"Not now," she murmured, reaching up to nuzzle under his chin. "There's a time for talking and this isn't one of them . . ."

And for once, Ned knew exactly what she meant. ■

take a sample!

This simply-stitched traditional sampler is brought to life with the addition of a ceramic, house-shaped button. If you prefer, the design could easily be worked on a 16-count Aida instead of the 32-count linen.

Stitch count
61 x 83

Design size
9.75 x 13.25 cm (3 ¾ x 5 ¼ in)

YOU WILL NEED

19.5 x 23.5 cm (7 ¾ x 9 ¼ in) Zweigart Belfast 32-count linen, shade 224 or 16-count cream Aida
Tapestry needle size 24
Stranded cotton (floss) as listed in chart key
Hand-crafted house button. Obtainable from most good needlework/craft shops, or contact Terata Ltd., Unit 8, Heath Business Centre, Heath Road, Hounslow, Middlesex TW3 2NF. Tel: 0208 230 3080

TIP
Take care that buttons, particularly wooden ones, do not mark your fabric. If unsure, coat the back with clear nail varnish before attaching.

1. Prepare the fabric by sewing a narrow hem around all raw edges to preserve the edges for hem stitching when the project is complete.

2. Fold the fabric in four and mark the folds with tacking (basting) stitches. Working over two fabric threads, use two strands of stranded cotton (floss) for cross stitches.

3. When the embroidery is complete, remove any tacking (basting). Use matching thread to stitch on the house button in the centre above the heart motif, and then mount and frame your work as a picture.

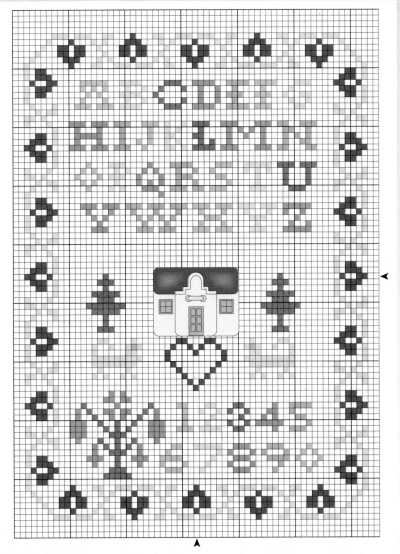

SAMPLER KEY Stranded Cotton (Floss)

DMC	ANCHOR					
223	10	420	1049	930	1036
315	65	832	307	3011	277
		926	208	3041	1018

sample this

Our square alphabet sampler would make a delightful picture.

Stitch count
78 x 75

Design Size
14 x 14cm (5 ½ x 5 ½ in)

YOU WILL NEED

24 x 24 cm (9 ½ x 9 ½ in) cream 16-count Aida
Tapestry needle size 24
Stranded cotton as listed in chart key (note: there is no DMC equivalent to Anchor 1335)

1. Prepare the fabric by sewing a narrow hem around all raw edges to preserve the edges for hem stitching when the project is complete.

2. Fold material in four to find centre and mark with tacking (basting) threads. Work design from the centre.
Use two strands of cotton for cross stitch and one for back stitch.

3. Remove tacking (basting) stitches, and then mount and frame your work as a picture.

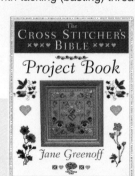

Taken from The Cross Stitcher's Bible Project Book by Jane Greenoff, published by David & Charles @ £17.99. You can order the book for the special price of £15.99 plus free p & p (UK mainland only). Call 01626 334555 and quote Y052.

Stranded Cotton (Floss)

	DMC	ANCHOR
	315	1019
	327	101

╲		1335
	930	922
	931	1034
	937	268
	3051	269

	3721	896
	3777	1015
	3821	874
◇	680	907

LAND OF
MY FATHERS

by Joyce Stranger

**The way of life her father had treasured was gone forever.
Even so, she was determined that whatever took its place
would be something he would be proud of . . .**

"Y OU should have come back before." Her brother's voice was
accusing. I should never have gone away. Eilie's thought was forlorn,
but she didn't say the words aloud.

She stood facing her brother Charles across the long table which held the
remains of the sandwiches and cakes that had eased the ending of her
father's funeral.

She'd flown halfway across the world and arrived too late. Too late to see
her father. Too late to tell him all she'd longed to say.

She looked at the picture John had painted for him, after the last ploughing match her father had won. John, whom she'd loved, but who was now no more than a regretful memory of what might have been . . .

"You ought to sell it," Charles said, following her gaze. "It's worth a fortune.

"Who would ever have thought that John would make it as anything, let alone an artist? He always seemed such a loser."

But he had kind eyes, and a gentle smile, and was everything she'd ever dreamed of . . . until she met Adam.

John's picture hung on the dining-room wall, above the huge brick fireplace. It evoked a pain that was worse than all the sorrow she hugged to her.

Fifteen years ago, when the picture was painted, she'd been a pony-tailed 15-year-old. John had been 18, yet already an accomplished artist. How she'd loved him . . .

Her father had been in his prime, and she'd adored him, loved watching him ploughing with Castor and Pollux, the two horses he'd treasured more than any he'd ever owned.

Time stood still in the picture. The farm was as it used to be, the lacy early spring trees shadowy against a burnished sky, the long furrows straight and true, rolling to the plough.

The two horses, their massive heads lowered, pulled against the tug of the heavy soil that resisted them.

She remembered the sound of the breaking waves and the sea piling into the land when the wind and the tide pulled together, and the far fields were awash.

She looked wistfully at the picture and wished she could go back — back to the days when she was young, and life was simple. But those days were far behind her now . . .

Adam had arrived at her father's farm as an exchange student when she was almost 20. He'd seemed so exciting, so full of life — and so different from the quiet, gentle John.

He'd won her heart with soft words and whispered promises, and she'd gladly agreed to become his wife. She'd gone back with him to his home in Australia, to the cattle station he'd described with such enthusiasm.

It had turned out to be little more than a derelict wooden house set amongst acres of parched ground, where it seldom rained and the water dried and the cattle died — and in time even her tears had dried, too, as she'd fought against fate and time and disaster.

And had lost . . .

Adam had been dead for two years, killed in a fall from a horse, when she'd decided to give up. She'd written to her father to say she was coming home and had sold the land that was left to her.

Then she'd flown back to England — but it had been too late to see her father again.

A heart attack, she was told — sudden and completely unexpected . . .

THE farmhouse was unchanged. So, too, was the big cobbled yard. The barns, the sties and the stables, the byres and the milking parlour, were reminders of more prosperous days.

The tiny cottage where her grandparents had lived was still as they'd left it, but looked forlorn and forgotten now.

She stared in disbelief at the housing estate that sprawled where once the horses had ploughed the sloping fields.

Nothing remained of the farm stock except for the two latest shires, Duchess and Prince, placid 12-year-olds who stood quietly in their stalls, tugging at haynets.

There was so much that she didn't understand.

"Why did he sell?" she demanded.

"I persuaded him to." Her brother Charles was a solid, heavy man, prosperous and pompous. She remembered him as a selfish boy, and he'd become a selfish man.

"It was for his own good. How could an old man manage two hundred acres alone? It was insane."

"Selling killed him!" Eilie thought of her father, and of the farm and animals he'd cherished, and of the misery he must have felt when he was left with a mere twelve acres of land.

"You always did over-dramatise things." Charles's voice was as cold and critical as she remembered it. He'd always been impatient with her.

"Dad would never have sold the land for a housing estate," she protested.

"It's there, isn't it? He can't have minded that much. Anyway, I have to get back. Alison will be expecting me. Will you be all right?"

It was a perfunctory question. As if he cared, Eilie thought, as she watched the silver Mercedes vanish down the road.

She was still bruised from the row that had broken out earlier that day when the will was read.

Nothing had been left to Charles. The farm and land and the animals were to go to Eilie. Charles had been furious.

They'd argued bitterly and now Charles had gone and she was alone in the old house.

Her room was as she'd left it, even to the battered teddy bear sitting on the shelf. She wandered through the rooms, remembering.

IT was dark outside now. Bright lights patched the estate where once the wide fields had lain, brown in winter, green in spring and then flushing to high summer gold.

Street lamps and house windows and people — hundreds of people. The houses blotted out the sound of the sea.

What had happened to the animals? Her father had written to her only a year ago about the geese, and the chickens, the new goats, and calves. Where were they all now?

She buried her grief in work. When every cup and plate and dish was put away, she brewed a cup of coffee and took some of the remaining sandwiches and a slice of cake and went into her father's study.

She couldn't bear to look at John's picture, to remember her father as he was then, or to remember John and the chance she'd thrown away. She'd fallen for the glitter and tossed away the gold.

The little bookcase was dusty. She brought a cloth and rubbed the wood until it shone.

Then she pulled out the photograph albums, and looked at herself as a toddler, and Charles as a small boy.

The press cuttings books were on the second shelf.

She picked them up, expecting to find cuttings of her father's wins at shows and in ploughing matches.

Instead, startled, she found herself reading a tale that filled her both with sadness and with rage.

The residents of the housing estate had produced petition after petition, complaining about her father's animals and way of life. Their complaints were all faithfully reported in the press. Her father had lost, every time.

The geese were unhygienic, it was claimed, and made far too much noise, so he was ordered to sell them. The cocks crowed at dawn and woke the estate, "disturbing the peace". Again he was ordered to get rid of them.

The list went on and on, each incident the same.

Eilie stared down at the book, so angry that her hands shook.

He might not have fought them, but they had her to reckon with now. How dared they dictate the way that others lived?

She returned to the cuttings, carefully pasted on to the grey pages.

The horses had broken the fence of a bungalow belonging to a Miss Summers, and there was an interview with her.

She'd spoken, eloquently, of the absurdity of those who lived in the past, and of an old man's stubborn refusal to sell the farm buildings as well as the land.

Eilie couldn't believe it, not any of it. What right had these incomers to insist upon changing a way of life that had endured for many hundreds of years?

She felt like an intruder, but she had to go through the rest of the papers, had to find out what was to be done.

There were plans in her father's desk for a promenade and a strengthened sea wall; for a little playground, and a park. Whatever had happened to those?

Then there was the letter he'd never posted.

My dearest Eilie,

I wish you could come home, though you wouldn't recognise the place now.

I sold most of the farmland, for a park and promenade, for space for people to walk, while still keeping my view of the sea.

I didn't want to, but Charles persuaded me, and the farm was getting too much for me to run on my own.

But the buyers sold out to property developers, and they've built an enormous housing estate on my land . . .

I found out that it was Charles's firm who'd originally bought the land, and then sold it to the developers.

He'd been trying to persuade me to sell for years, but I never thought he would trick me like that.

He made a fortune when he sold on, which is why I'm leaving him nothing.

You will inherit all that I have. Maybe you'll want to sell, but at least the money won't go to Charles, who deceived his own father.

The letter ended there, unfinished, and unsigned.

That night, Eilie was unable to sleep.

Her anger returned with daylight and the sight of the estate.

It drove her through the next week, as she cleaned the house and washed curtains and blankets and carpets, trying to kill grief with action.

And then the letter arrived . . .

The writer was her father's persecutor, Miss Summers. She hoped that Eilie would honour her father's promise, and sell the horses, which didn't belong in a built-up area.

Twelve acres was hardly built-up! Eilie tore the letter to shreds.

Who did this woman think she was? The newspaper named her as being the instigator of the petitions to have the animals removed.

They'd badgered him to death — but now they had her to reckon with.

Eilie drove out in the Land Rover and bought 20 laying hens and put them in the enclosure. Later she would buy a cockerel and have live chicks of her own.

It was a way of living. The estate wouldn't like it, but she didn't care.

Miss Summers wrote again — and again.

She discovered that Eilie had bought a puppy and a kitten and called round on some pretext to have a look at the yard.

She was a tall, thin woman, with cold grey eyes and an uncompromising stare. And it took all Eilie's restraint not to order her off the property.

SPRING flared to high summer and then the good weather ended. Savage winds tormented the woods, and high seas battered against the coast. Daily, the rain lashed down; gales tore tiles from roofs and felled branches.

Eilie could hear the surging roar of the angry seas, even with the houses in the way. The farm was on a high knoll, protected by thickly growing trees.

One night in early September, Eilie woke up and got dressed. She'd never heard such a storm.

The wind howled around the house, rattling doors and windows, terrifying the puppy and the kitten, who hid under her bed.

She read until the lights went out, when the power lines were brought down.

She heard the agitated hooves of both horses thunder against their stable wall, but the kitchen door slammed shut as she struggled to open it.

Roof tiles smashed on the cobbles in the yard and she knew that, even if she did manage to get outside, she'd never be able to stand.

She'd never heard such turmoil. All she could do was sit and wait, and hope that the storm would blow itself out.

Morning brought calm in the skies — and chaos on the ground.

Sheets of roofing felt, torn from the byres, littered the fields. Trees lay broken where, the night before, they'd stood tall.

As she walked to the stables she looked down towards the estate. She couldn't believe that the tidy streets had vanished overnight.

The white fingers of the sea were clawing at the edge of the knoll where the farm stood.

A cat sat, terrified, on a roof that stood only a few feet above the water.

There were boats where cars had once driven.

She stared for a moment in horror, then raced across the yard and harnessed the shires.

Riding Duchess and leading Prince, she trotted across the fields into what had once been a back garden.

She grabbed a child from its mother's arms, as the woman held him out of a window.

She handed him to a policeman, an extraordinary sight, sitting as he was in a brightly-painted rowing-boat. The mother followed, using Prince's back as a stepping stone.

"Can you stay? We need as much help as we can get," the policeman said, steering his passengers towards safety.

She spent the rest of the day, soaked and weary, helping lift people down from the backs of the horses into the boats that plied busily everywhere.

"We haven't been able to get to the end bungalow," one of the policemen said. "The front is blocked by a pile of wooden planks from broken sheds. Could you get round the back?"

The horses waded, almost chest deep, while Eilie pushed debris out of the way with a sturdy plank.

It was a long way, and they had to detour several times to avoid hidden obstacles.

She was afraid of the power and strength of the sea, of the remorseless thrust of water all around them, pushing at the once trim bungalows, drowning the gardens, swallowing everything it touched.

The wind was rising, beating the sea to froth, but still the horses plodded on.

MISS SUMMERS was standing on her dining-room table, watching the sea rise all around her. Her possessions floated, whirling in the eddies.

"You'll have to wade!" Eilie yelled above the sound of the sea, and watched as her one-time adversary struggled across to the window, pushed it open and climbed out on to the sill.

She stared at the waves, only inches below her.

Eilie's hand reached down, hauling the woman on to Prince's broad back.

They sat for a moment, looking at the remnants of yesterday's homes, and then the two shires turned and thrust through the wind-tossed waves, Eilie guiding them towards higher ground.

"All right, miss?" The policeman was soaked, his boat crowded with an unlikely crew of people.

"We'll live. I'll take Miss Summers home with me. You must have too many people to find room for."

"We have. And it won't be just for a day or two, either. When the sea goes back . . ." He left the words unsaid.

Drowned floors and broken furnishings; soaked walls and soil washed into houses. No electricity and punctured gas mains.

Devastation and destruction everywhere.

Eilie shivered in the icy wind.

Miss Summers gripped Prince's mane, fear of the horse almost as strong as the fear of the sea. Her soaked clothes outlined her lean body, and her hair clung to her face.

She'd lost all dignity and was only a tired woman, homeless and terrified.

Eilie's anger died.

The farmhouse was mercifully dry and warm, braced against the winds, sheltering under the trees. Eilie led her unexpected guest into the kitchen.

"I have to go out and dry the horses. There's plenty of hot water. If you go upstairs and look in the room at the top of the staircase you'll find some of my father's clothes — mine won't fit you. Best to take those wet things off as soon as possible."

Outside in the stable she rubbed down the two shires.

She dried them as best she could, and spread the straw thick and deep. She filled the mangers and their buckets and haynets.

Only then was she free to dry herself, to soak wearily in hot water, and thank heaven for her own security.

Miss Summers had drawn the curtains, and shut out the desolate view. She sat, nursing a steaming mug of coffee. Another mug waited for Eilie.

"Your father knew," the older woman said abruptly. "I thought he was making it up, just to be tiresome. He stormed out of that first meeting, shouting that the sea would take its revenge. We thought he was being vindictive because we'd won.

"He knew that the waves would come in. He said that the land here always flooded in the spring and autumn tides, and that every hundred years or so the sea raided the land.

"He fought us, and we fought back, selfishly, wanting our homes, and sure he only wanted to stop us building so near to his farm."

"A hundred years ago," Eilie echoed. Suddenly, she was a small girl again, sitting in the kitchen, listening to her elders.

"My great-grandmother was still at school then. The sea came in, almost up to the edge of the knoll. There was only farmland then — no homes to destroy." Eilie remembered her grandmother telling her the story.

"You'd think people would remember," Miss Summers protested. "Why didn't the developers think?"

"A hundred years is a long time," Eilie said. So is ten, she thought. In ten years the houses had been built — and had been taken away by the sea.

NEXT morning the two women stood side by side, looking down from the knoll.

The receding tide had left seaweed and devastation in its wake. People walked among the debris, visiting their homes, lost and forlorn.

"I feel as if everything and everyone I knew has died," Miss Summers said, as Eilie dished up breakfast for both of them.

"I felt like that when I came back," Eilie said. "My father dead, and the farm broken up. Just that tiny piece of land left." She looked up at John's painting.

"That was my father when he was young — with Castor and Pollux, his favourite horses. That's the big field. It sloped down the hill and then gave way to the sea.

"My family have lived here for nearly two hundred years, you know."

"You won't sell?"

"No, I won't sell. I want to build the farm up again, though there's little enough left.

"Maybe I could open it to the public, for children to visit — and to learn from. I want to bring the animals back.

"A world without animals is unthinkable."

Eilie hadn't realised, until that moment, just what she intended to do, but now that she'd said it she knew it was right. Her father would have approved.

There was a long silence between the two women. Then Miss Summers spoke, her voice hesitant and unsure.

"I think you're right. I think we all have to learn to live with each other, not fight all the time.

"I'd like to help," she went on, taking Eilie by surprise. "That cottage at the side of the yard — would you rent it to me?"

Eilie stared at her, unsure of what to say.

"I spent the night awake, thinking about how wrong I was," the older woman explained. "Your father was right. Nature is more powerful than people and we have to learn to live with that, not to impose our will.

"We can't win, not against the wind and the storm and the sea. I'd lost sight of that."

She stared up at the picture, as if she were talking to the man who looked down on her, from his position beside the horses.

"I had so much to do, so much of interest, when I was working. I was a teacher, you see. All those children to watch grow up and develop and go out into the world.

"I loved my job, and they were the children I never had."

Eilie, watching her, felt a sudden wave of pity.

"And then one day you have to retire and there's nothing to occupy you at all. Endless hours feeling as if you've been thrown on a scrap heap."

"Endless days which you filled by trying to make my father see that you stood for progress, and he stood for the past." Eilie began to understand.

"I thought that was what I was doing, but last night I discovered I was wrong. Everything I owned has gone. I have nothing left — nothing at all."

"You're insured?"

"I'm insured, but I won't ever live there again. I'd be afraid, all the time.

"I'd hear the sea, always teasing the edge of the beach, and it would terrify me in the long, sleepless nights. Clawing at the land, waiting to invade again."

"I want to bring the animals back," Eilie said again. "The farm has no life without them. I want to breed shire horses. I want pigs in the sties again — and cocks crowing in the yard.

"I want to open the farm to visitors, to show them how people live in the country.

"We grow the food; you all depend on us. On men like my father.

"If I let you have the cottage, will you leave the farm alone? No-one is going to make me sell up."

"I had a long time to think, when the waters were rising all around me." Miss Summers looked at the kitten curled up on the rug.

"I had a cat as a child, but my father made me give her away, because he said she was unhygienic. I never let myself get fond of any animal again."

She picked up the kitten and hugged it to her, her eyes bright with tears.

Later that day the two women put the little cottage in the yard to rights.

Then Eilie took the kitten to the cottage.

"We'll have too many animals to cope with soon," she said. "I promised we'd take the ones from the estate until homes can be found for everyone. The kitten's yours, if you want her."

"It's strange," Miss Summers began. "It's almost as if I've shed some kind of shell that stopped me from enjoying life. Tomorrow, it's a new beginning."

"And for me, too," Eilie said. "There's so much to be done. I have to bring life back to the farm."

She saw the future, with the land brown and sweet, and the wild white gulls flying. The memories of the stark and barren years would fade.

She looked up at her father's picture, remembering John with regret, but not with bitterness.

The farm would live again. She thought she saw a smile cross the pictured face and knew that she had, indeed, come home. ■

I put flowers on your grave today.
It's ten years since you went away.
Words unsaid and thoughts untold.
I regret that now I'm old.
I walked home down the lonely street.
Then thought, high time I had a treat,
A sudden yearning to re-capture,
Forgotten days of courting rapture.
I walked beside the waterfall.
Then I heard the river's call.
Long ago beneath the trees,
Our hair was ruffled by the breeze.
"Look," you said.
A white swan, gliding
In the reeds, an otter, hiding.
Sunlight on the water stippling,
White waves against the bank were rippling.
But you are gone. The surface bare,
There is no white swan sailing there.
Do otters still come here and play,
Or have they also gone away?
The water's grey as any stone
And I am sitting here, alone.
Then comes a sudden sapphire flash,
Jewelled feathers dive, a silver splash.
The sight you longed for, never saw.
He never did come here before.
I do so wish that you'd been there
That moment of delight to share.
The sun has gone, the bird has flown
But even though I'm on my own,
I've a new thought I can treasure,
That such rare sights can still bring pleasure.

The Kingfisher

A poem by Joyce
Stranger, inspired by
an illustration
by Mark Viney.

Our Country Cottage

by Josefine Beaumont

It was a dream come true for the family — and a nightmare for me!

IT all started when my Great-Aunt Edie decided to go into a home for the elderly. She phoned me with the news and I could hardly believe my ears. Edie had always been fiercely independent, and she loved her home and garden.

"Are you sure it's what you want?" I asked doubtfully.

"Perfectly," came her crisp reply. "I'm eighty-nine, Victoria. It's time I was looked after. And I've had a look round Greenacres. I was most impressed."

I wasn't. I knew Edie. In the past, she'd often insisted that she'd never go into a home.

"There's something you're not telling me!" I accused her, and there was a silence before she replied apologetically, "Well, to tell the truth, dear, I haven't been feeling up to the mark since my hip replacement operation."

It took a moment or two for her words to sink in and then I shrieked, "Hip replacement operation! You had an operation and didn't tell me? Oh, Edie . . .!"

"What was the point?" she rejoined. "You'd only have worried."

"That's it," I declared. "You're not going into a home, Edie. I won't hear of it. You'll come and live with us."

"Thank you, dear, but no," she said gently. "I'm grateful, I really am. But you see, I just couldn't live in a city, Victoria. I'd hate it. And I'd feel like a burden. You know how much I'd hate that."

Yes, I did, she'd told me often enough.

"Besides," she went on. "Greenacres really is a wonderful place.

"I'll have a lovely room overlooking the rose gardens, and I'll be able to take some of my own bits and pieces with me. It's what I want, dear. Really it is."

Tears filled my eyes. It seemed to me that a chapter of her life had closed forever. I suddenly felt so very sad for her.

"I just want you to be happy, Edie," I sniffed and she laughed and assured me, "Oh, I will be, don't worry.

"Now then, dear," she continued briskly, "about the house. I want you to have it. In fact, I've already talked to my solicitor about it."

"Oh, no, Edie, I couldn't accept —" I began, but she interrupted me. "Why ever not? It'll be yours one day anyway."

"Don't say things like that!" I said crossly, and she laughed again.

"I just want to see you properly settled, dear," she told me.

"You could sell it," I suggested. "Cottages like yours are worth a fortune these days, you know. You'd have no problem, I'm sure of it."

"Oh, I know that," she replied airily. "The solicitor's already told me that. He said the puppies . . . or was it the groupies . . . would snap up a cottage like mine."

"Yuppies," I corrected her, smiling in spite of my worries.

"Whatever," she rejoined. "Anyway, I told him I wasn't interested. I want you and Sam and the children to have a proper home of your own. I hate to think of you all squashed together in that flat.

"It must be hard for you, dear. Let me do this one last thing for you."

I had trouble holding back my tears when she said that.

"I love you, Edie, you know that, don't you? And . . . and thank you."

"That's what life's all about, Victoria." Her voice was suddenly gentle. "It's about loving people, dear."

And that's how we came to live in Dovecote Cottage . . .

I'LL be honest. At first, the very thought of living in a small village made my heart sink.

I was a city girl, born and bred — I liked the bright lights, the shops, cinemas and theatres that surrounded us, and the constant hum of people.

But I found myself outnumbered. I couldn't find it in my heart to refuse Edie's more than generous offer. And then the reaction of my family really sealed my fate . . .

"Can we have a dog, Mum? Please?" eleven-year-old Lee pleaded desperately.

"I'd love a cat. Can I have a cat, Mum?" nine-year-old Craig implored, lifting shining eyes to mine.

"I want a rabbit. I've always wanted a rabbit, Mum. Like the ones we have at school. I'll call it Cherries," six-year-old Karen decided, determined not to be outdone.

"Just think," Sam, my husband, said emotionally. "We'll have a garden of our own. Somewhere for the kids to play, without us having to worry about the roads.

"I'll be able to grow my own veg. I've always wanted a garden. I can't believe it, Vicky. We'll never be able to thank Edie for this."

Dogs? Cats? Rabbits? Vegetables? I felt faint. I groped for a chair and sank down into it, my eyes taking in the superb fitted kitchen we'd scrimped and saved and waited four years for.

I suddenly remembered Edie's antiquated kitchen. The one with the chipped stone sink and the old iron stove that belched black smoke.

And finally, but fatally, I remembered the bathroom. The one that didn't exist. Unless, that is, you counted the sagging wooden hut that sat at the bottom of the garden.

"Isn't it great!" Sam hugged me.

"Great," I agreed faintly.

WHOEVER said that moving house was one of the top three most stressful situations knew what he was talking about.

By the time the last of the boxes had been carried into the cottage, my nerves were stretched as tight as an overworked elastic band.

I fell into bed that night and lay in an exhausted huddle. But did I sleep? No, I did not. I'd always thought that the country was quiet, but it isn't. I've never heard so many squeaks and groans and odd noises in all my life.

"What's that?" I kept hissing at Sam, sitting bolt upright in bed and fearfully clutching the duvet close to my chest. But I was wasting my time. He slept right through it all.

Four days later, we became the proud owners of one huge and hairy dog from the local pound. He was the size of a horse and ate like one, too. And he never did a thing he was told.

Of course, having provided Lee with his longed-for dog, we naturally had to provide Craig with his longed-for cat.

Horatio slept all day and prowled all night and thought the living-room furniture had been provided especially for him to sharpen his claws on.

But even I couldn't complain about Karen's rabbit, Cherries. He was adorable!

Sam and I worked out that by next April we'd be able to afford to turn the box room into a bathroom. Until then we had to make do with washing in an old tin bath in front of the fire.

Oddly enough, I rather enjoyed my bath nights. I'd lie in the hot water, the warmth of the coal fire gently fanning me, and luxuriate in the peace and quiet.

Sam made a point of taking the kids out for a walk so that I could enjoy my soak without interruptions.

But one evening, as I lay in scented water up to my chin, I heard an insistent scratching noise.

I stiffened. What could scratch like that?

Mice, that's what! And I mean mice, not a mouse.

Where there's a mouse you can be sure its wife and children, aunts and uncles, grannies and grandpas and nephews and nieces are not far behind.

I turned rigid with terror.

I looked longingly at the door leading to the hall. It was only about six feet away. Surely I could leap that far . . . couldn't I?

With an ear-piercing shriek, I threw myself into the hall, clutching my towel around me and dripping all over the carpet. That's when Sam and the kids trooped in.

"It's raining cats and dogs out there," Sam commented cheerfully. "We're in for a storm by the looks of things." Then, catching sight of my disarray, he exclaimed. "Vicky! What on earth are you doing?"

"M . . . m . . . mice!" I managed to stutter.

"Mice?" He frowned. "Where?"

"In — in the k . . . kitchen, Sam . . ."

"Mice!" Lee yelled excitedly, beaming at Craig. "Yippee!" And with that they darted gleefully into the kitchen, Karen hot on their heels.

"I'll get rid of them," Sam vowed. "But you know, Vicky, you shouldn't be frightened of mice. They're more afraid of you than you are of them."

"No, Sam, they're not!" I said, my voice dangerously low.

"Oh, I nearly forgot!" he exclaimed, changing the subject. "I bought you a present in the village." My spirits lifted. Maybe it was a bottle of my favourite perfume. But my spirits plummeted again when he handed me a huge bag. Perfume doesn't come in huge bags.

Wellies do, though!

I BURST into tears and fled upstairs, Sam following close behind. "What's the matter?" he demanded.

"Nothing!" I sniffed.

"You're not happy!" he accused.

"I am!" I lied.

"You're not!"

"I want to go home!" I wailed.

As soon as the words had left my mouth, I wished I hadn't said them.

Sam's face fell, and I felt terrible. I knew he loved it here — and the kids did, too.

"We are home," he said, but I didn't reply.

"We can't sell this house, Vicky," he said dully. "You know how much it means to Aunt Edie . . ." His voice trailed away and my shame overwhelmed me.

"I know," I said wearily, thinking of how much she had loved the cottage. "I'm just tired, Sam, that's all."

Just then there was a rumble of thunder, and the sky was lit up for a brief second by a sheet of lightning. Rain beat against the window panes and I peered out into the garden.

"You were right about the storm," I said. "And you've left your gardening shoes outside. You'd better bring them in. They'll be wet through."

Sam left the room without a word. He was back within minutes, his face as white as a sheet.

"Vicky!" he whispered urgently.

"What is it?" I crossed the room and grasped his arm. "What's the matter?"

"You —" he swallowed hard, "— you won't believe this, but . . . but I brought my shoes in and put them in the hall and . . . and, well, one shoe moved."

"Moved?" I stared at him. "What do you mean, moved?"

"It moved!" he hissed. "All on its own."

"It can't have!"

"It did!"

"Don't be silly. You must have imagined it."

"I didn't, Vicky. In fact, it — it moved a few times. Honestly."

Our eyes met and, of like mind, we made for the door together. Halfway down the stairs we came to a standstill and stared at the shoes. And then suddenly, before my disbelieving eyes, one shoe shuffled forwards.

I nearly fainted clean away!

"I told you!" Sam hissed.

I don't believe in ghosts, I told myself firmly, but for all that I shook Sam's arm and gasped frantically, "The children!"

He scuttled down the stairs, with me cowering behind him, neither of us taking our eyes off that shoe.

And then, before our very eyes, one of the biggest and ugliest toads it has ever been my misfortune to look upon suddenly leapt out of the shoe. It must have hidden in there during the storm.

I jumped back in terror — but I didn't jump as far as Sam. With a sudden squeak he was behind me. His face had turned a very peculiar shade of green and he gasped, "I hate toads!"

That's when I started to laugh.

I laughed until the tears rolled down my face. I laughed until the noise brought the kids dashing into the hall to see what all the excitement was about. I laughed until I couldn't stand any more and had to sit down on the bottom step.

Sam cowered four steps above me, quaking in his size elevens.

"Wow! A toad!" Craig shouted, pointing excitedly.

"Quick, catch it!" Lee yelled.

"It's there! It's there!" Karen shrieked.

It was Lee who eventually caught the toad. He held it gently in the palm of his hand and stroked its scaly back.

"Isn't it great, Mum?" he asked lovingly.

I looked into the bright and happy faces of my children, and something warm and wonderful stole over me.

"Great!" I agreed cheerfully, thinking of how much Edie would have loved all this.

"There aren't any mice, Mum," Craig said woefully, remembering the earlier adventure. "It was a bird trapped in the pantry. We let it out of the window."

I looked up to where Sam stood shuddering on the stairs and said slyly, "You know, Sam, you shouldn't be frightened of a toad. It's more afraid of you than you are of it."

"That's not funny, Vicky!" he said stiffly — and started me laughing all over again.

"My hero!" I gasped.

GREAT-AUNT EDIE thoroughly approved of all the renovations we made to the cottage. She particularly liked the new bathroom, and she adored the fitted kitchen. But then so did I.

We've lived in Dovecote Cottage for almost eight years now. How time has flown!

Sadly, we lost Edie five years ago. She passed away peacefully in her sleep and, oh, how we miss her! We were all heartbroken and weekends just aren't the same without her.

I'll never sell this house, though. It's hard to believe I ever wanted to leave it at all, because this is my home.

Within these four walls we have lived and laughed and created wonderful memories that we will each carry forever.

No, I'll never sell this house now . . .

And sometimes, when a shaft of sunlight streams through the window, or when the rain beats against the roof, I think of Edie and smile.

I think of the gift she gave me — not only this house, but the other gift, the one beyond price. Because bricks and mortar alone don't make a home. It's the people who do, working together for a good, decent life.

That's what life's about — loving people. And that's what Edie taught me. That was her last gift to me. ■

AFTER MIDNIGHT

— by Isobel Stewart —

It was silly to worry... but it was getting late to be out on a first date...

I SAID I wouldn't wait up for her. But it's almost midnight, and here I am in the kitchen, in my old blue dressing-gown, with milk ready to heat for hot chocolate as soon as she comes home.

I'll be very casual, of course.

"Have a nice time?" I'll ask. And: "No, I didn't wait up — I said I wouldn't . . . but I woke five minutes ago, so I just came down."

We'll both know that isn't true, but she won't say.

I'll know right away how her date has been. Because I've seen her go off before, so happily, so hopefully, looking so pretty, smiling so brightly.

Too brightly? I've wondered, sometimes.

It's so hard, loving someone and knowing that loving means letting go. I keep having this ridiculous urge to protect her, to keep her from getting hurt.

But I can't do that, I know that I have to let her face her own hurts, and learn to live with them.

She seems so vulnerable, so alone. I know that isn't how other people see her. Independent — able to look after herself — a survivor. I've heard people say that about her.

I know she isn't really like that, though.

For so long, there's been just the two of us. I've seen her when her confidence has been low.

We've cried together, not often, because she wants to be strong, for me, but enough for me to know that she's had to fight to achieve that bright independence, and sometimes she needs to let it fade just a little.

But it's time now to forget yesterday, and to think of today and tomorrow. We both know that. And so I have to let her go.

I have to learn to live my own life, to stand on my own feet, and so does she.

Only . . . I don't want her to be hurt.

The last time she went out on a date, she'd come to my room just before she left.

"How do I look?" she asked me — her voice very light, very bright.

"Fine," I told her, truthfully. I hesitated, and then I asked very casually — I've become quite good at being casual — "Someone special?"

"Oh no," she'd said quickly. "Just a date, that's all." She shrugged. "Maybe we'll get on well, maybe we'll want to see each other again. Maybe not. No big deal."

I knew it wasn't a big deal, but I knew, too, that it was important for her to be able to feel confident and good about herself.

That night I went to bed before she came home, but I couldn't sleep. And I think I knew how things had worked out, by the sound of her footsteps as she came upstairs.

"You asleep?" she'd said softly, at the door of my room. Her voice was light.

"No — at least I was, but I'm awake now." And casual again, "Nice evening?"

"Very nice. That French film is terrific. You should try to see it if you can."

So we'd talked about the French film and I didn't need to ask if she would be seeing him again, because I sensed from the way she spoke that she wouldn't.

Men! I think now, as I sit in the kitchen listening to the clock in the hall chime twelve. There are times when you feel you could shake them.

It's not that she wants or needs a Big Romance. Right now, all she needs is to know that someone finds her attractive, enjoys her company, and wants to see her again.

You wouldn't think that was too much to ask, would you?

She hasn't been this late before and, although I'm anxious, I can't help hoping it's a good sign. I only saw him for five minutes, when he came to pick her up, but I liked him. He was quite ordinary, really, but had a nice smile.

"I promise I won't keep her out too late," he said to me as they left.

I felt a bit embarrassed, because I was trying not to seem anxious or fussy, and he'd obviously seen through that. But he smiled then, and somehow I didn't feel so bad.

I like him, I thought, and that surprised me, because I'm usually cautious about judging people. And at the same time, I thought that she seemed different, somehow, on this date. Less anxious, less tense — more relaxed, more herself.

I HEAR a car draw up, and suddenly I think — what if she brings him in for coffee? Me here in my old dressing-gown, with the milk ready to heat — I might spoil everything!

But before I can run upstairs, I hear them at the door. They are talking softly, and then I hear them both laughing. Then some more talking, and the door opens, and I hear his footsteps going back down the path.

She must be standing at the door, waiting to wave goodbye to him, I realise. Then the car door closes, and the car drives off, and she closes the front door and comes through.

"Hi," she says, smiling, and my heart gives a funny little lurch, because I know that it's all right.

"You shouldn't have waited up," she says then, gently, and she puts her arms around me as I sit there at the kitchen table.

This time, I don't pretend that I didn't wait up.

"I thought you'd like some hot chocolate," I say, and I get up and heat the milk.

When I put the two mugs of hot chocolate down on the table, she's sitting down, and she's smiling.

"I like him," I say abruptly.

"So do I," she replies. And then, cautiously — "We did get on well together. He's very easy to talk to, but, well, I don't know what I'm trying to say."

She pushes her hand through her hair, and suddenly she looks much younger.

"One swallow doesn't make a summer?" I suggest.

She thinks about that, as she drinks her hot chocolate.

"I'm not really looking for summer, you know," she says after a while. Then she smiles. "Just a hint of spring, at this stage."

That's right, I think, surprised. That's exactly it. That's all she wants, right now, and all I want for her. Just a hint of spring. And somehow, looking at her, I have a sudden certainty that she's got it.

"You mustn't worry so much about me," she says now, taking me by surprise, because I've always thought I'd done a pretty good job of hiding that.

"I don't worry about you," I say, completely untruthfully.

She raises her eyebrows.

"Well, if a girl can't worry a bit about her mother when she starts dating again, it's a poor show!" I tell her.

She stands up.

"Time we were both in bed," she says firmly. "College for you tomorrow, and work for me."

She rinses the mugs, and leaves them to drain, and we walk upstairs together.

"Maybe next time I go out with John," she says, and she smiles, "you won't feel you have to wait up for me!"

Next time. I like the sound of that, I think.

"Maybe," I agree.

At the top of the stairs, we kiss goodnight, my mother and I. ■

To Be My Own Woman

by Teresa Ashby

Strangely enough, I owed my new-found independence to someone else!

SATURDAY is Market Day and Hangwell, which is normally quiet and unremarkable, becomes a bustling metropolis, filled to bursting point with trolley-dragging, buggy-pushing, carrier-bag-laden humanity.

Looking for a needle in a haystack has nothing on trying to find a parking space in Hangwell on Market Day, and finding a shop without a queue half a mile long would be like stumbling upon an oasis in the Sahara.

All I'd wanted was a small bag of potting compost — instead I found myself with a large problem.

The door of Gardens, Pets 'n' Ponds clanged shut behind me and I stood for a moment on the pavement outside, shell-shocked, as the Saturday shoppers pushed and jostled by.

I fought my way to the back street where I'd managed to squash the car in between a skip loaded with rubble and a "J" reg estate car loaded with "I've-Been-To" stickers. It wasn't until I was actually sitting behind the wheel that the enormity of what I'd done hit me.

Here and now, in this quiet back street, I had time to reflect on the stupidity of my actions.

I had come out of the shop with my arms full, but without my precious potting compost!

I bit my lip and looked at the box on the passenger seat beside me. Why had I done it?

Impulsive — it was a better word to use than stupid, but either would do.

Someone in an old banger crammed with kids hooted. They wanted my parking space.

The woman behind the wheel had that kind of desperate look on her face that said, "I've been driving around this town for two hours and if I don't park soon, I'm going to die!"

I waved and moved on. After all, the sooner I got home, the better.

She waved gratefully and while she was doing that, a man drove straight into my vacated space.

I lost sight of them as I turned the corner and couldn't afford to wonder what would happen next.

I had more pressing concerns.

A month ago, three things had happened to change my life.

First, my divorce was finalised after 19 years of marriage. Nineteen years since I, a dewy-eyed and heavily-pregnant teenager, had been practically frog-marched into the local registry office by my mother.

My dad had looked upset and kept blowing his nose and taking deep, unhappy breaths.

Mother had been too excited at the prospect of becoming a granny to be too upset.

Anyway, all that happened 19 years ago — and I was telling you about last month.

The second thing that happened was that I moved house. Everything in our four-bedroomed family house had to be divided two ways.

The things I had considered half mine for more than half my life, were suddenly his.

My bookcase, his books, my cookery books, his wok, my dressing table, his antique mirror.

It was all very amicable and civilised, I'm pleased to say. We'd passed the violent, reactive stage by then.

My new place — a cottage on the end of a terrace of four — had two bedrooms, a big garden and a hole with a roof in it.

I spent the first night moving my bed from one end of the bedroom to the other, trying to find a double-bed-sized patch which would keep me reasonably dry.

I'd ended up in tears, wondering why I had been brought to this while my ex-husband had moved upmarket into an even bigger house, with his exciting new girlfriend.

It all seemed so unfair, especially when none of it had been remotely my fault — not at all.

Thirdly, and perhaps the most shattering change of all, had been the departure of the twins.

Oh, didn't I mention that?

The bump which had accompanied me to my wedding became two — Craig and Gary — both at university now.

Craig was at Leeds, while Gary was at Cambridge. Clever boys both of them — unlike me!

With them gone, I knew I'd have to find something to do with my time or go mad, so I took up delivering the local free newspaper and reading manuscripts for a small local publisher.

I wasn't ready for the outside world just yet. I wanted to lower myself into it gradually, bit by bit, the way you walk into the sea when it's icy cold.

AFTER my frantic trip to Hangwell, I was relieved to get home and, as usual, admire my new roof. It was one problem I'd sorted, although hardly a day passed when I didn't find another.

And somehow, today, I'd managed to create a brand-new one which was as far removed from leaky roofs, burst pipes and fizzling electric sockets as possible.

Max was in the back garden fixing the fence. He's a self-employed handyman and I don't know how I'd have managed without him.

"Could you put a plug on this new kettle for me?" I called out. "Then I'll make some coffee."

He straightened up and scratched his head. There was a brown, iron-shaped mark on the chest of his T-shirt, the rest of it was creased and crumpled.

He frowned, rubbed his head a bit more, then said, "Be there in a minute," and got back to his fence mending.

I put the box on the floor of my cosy sitting-room and carefully opened it.

A head popped up. It belonged to the ugliest kitten I'd ever seen in my life!

Striped, with huge feet, he had an expression in his pale green eyes which could only be described as permanently startled.

His purr was loud, nasal and, the happier he got, the more he dribbled.

He didn't smell very pleasant, either!

He was the kind of animal all the experts advise you not to buy.

He'd been found on the docks, one of a litter of five.

Three were dead, one had found a home already and I had the ugly one. His mother was assumed dead.

I'd passed the wire cage, determined not to look inside as I entered the combined pet and garden supplies shop, but he'd reached out a white-socked paw to me.

"He's an ugly little beggar, isn't he?" the man in the pet shop said. "I can't see that one finding a home."

The kitten sat in his wire cage watching me with those startled eyes and I said, "I'll take him!"

I'd bought all the equipment, too. A litter tray, litter, kitten food and a catnip mouse — oh, and a book about cats.

My husband hadn't approved of pets.

The boys had never had that longed-for puppy and I still carried the guilt around with me, because I hadn't had the guts to disagree with their father.

Naming the kitten was easy — Theo! It was a rather grand name for such a sad creature, but he seemed to like it.

In the vet's the following morning, I sat with him zipped inside my jacket with just his pink nose and startled eyes peeping out.

I came away with my pockets bulging.

I had worm pills, flea powder for him, flea spray for the house, drops for his ears and ointment for his eyes.

He'd had the first of his vaccinations and had already cost me a small fortune.

"He smells," the vet had told me, "because he doesn't appear to know how to groom. Very sad."

THE stripey fur grew daily more dingy, though he was soon clear of fleas and his ears were now clean.

Ugly, loveable, house-trained and smelly, I had no choice but to bath him in the sink.

Cats do not, as a rule, like water, and Theo was no exception.

He shot out of the sink into my arms, clawed his way down my body and sped into the bedroom.

I found him beneath the rug under the bed. He emerged smellier and dirtier than ever.

He slept, not in the cosy wicker basket I'd bought him, but on my pillow, and usually woke me by patting my nose with his paw, claws carefully tucked away.

I was growing to love him, but his total lack of personal hygiene was driving a wedge between us.

Allowing Theo out into the outside world was as nerve-racking and alarming as the first time you wave a child off on its own.

I followed him around the garden, pretending to be occupied, but ready to grab him the minute he made for the front garden and the road.

He made his way around like a feline commando, starting off beneath a rose bush, then bounding to the shelter of a lilac, before darting into the cover of long grass.

It was a passing butterfly which finally brought him out of hiding.

He sat up on his haunches, patting the air with his front paws, those startled eyes flicking from side to side as the butterfly danced just out of reach.

Then he saw a bird.

Carrying himself low to the ground, he advanced with all the skill and expertise of a much older cat.

The ability to wash himself may not have been instinctive, but the hunting technique certainly was.

Fortunately, the blackbird was more skilled in cat-evasion than Theo was in bird-catching and when Theo pounced, the bird soared, but there was a look in Theo's eyes which said, "Next time!" and I didn't doubt that he meant it.

The cat flap came next, then the mice — three of them, one dead, two very much alive!

Dear Theo, sitting in the middle of the kitchen, had saved them for me, as though he knew how much I'd enjoy chasing them, catching them and eating them.

I obliged as far as the first two were concerned, but my gratitude ended there!

I released the mice in the garden, advised them to make themselves scarce and went inside to have a word with Theo.

★ ★ ★ ★

Remarkably, the ugly little kitten grew with almost indecent speed — but he still had a hygiene problem.

Or, rather, I did, for I couldn't give him a cuddle without ending up smelly myself.

It was Max who suggested a possible solution. Max, indeed, had solved most of my problems.

He'd fixed the roof, the pipes, and had seen to the rewiring. He'd also fitted the cat flap.

We'd become friends over the past few months. I guess we had a lot in common.

Max's wife had run off with his best friend and next-door neighbour, who also happened to be his boss.

So he'd somehow wound up losing his wife, his home and his job all in one go.

Max was . . . very different from my ex.

Tall, rangy, with wide shoulders, blue eyes and a ready smile, he was a hotch potch, a mongrel, not the most handsome man in the world, but, like Theo, oddly appealing.

I'd taken my first step into the outside world by this time in the form of a job as school secretary at our local primary school.

"Get another cat!" Max said. "It will show Theo how to keep clean."

"Theo wouldn't like that," I said, but, mentally, I was listing all the reasons my ex would have given for not having another cat.

Max, sprawled untidily in a chair in the conservatory, grinned and continued tickling Theo's ears.

Eventually, he said, "Try it. If it doesn't work, I'll take the new moggy off your hands."

★ ★ ★ ★

If Theo was the tough-guy alley cat, then Desmond was an aristocrat.

Half Siamese, he was elegant, beautiful and sophisticated.

His pale fawn-coloured fur was velvety and his eyes a vivid blue colour, but he seemed to have no cat-sense at all.

Theo hated him on sight but, within a week, they were inseparable.

Theo watched the kitten wash himself, puzzled, then looked at me and seemed to shrug.

It took a few weeks for him to catch on, but eventually the penny dropped and Theo's grey fur slowly became lighter and the pong began to vanish.

Theo taught Desmond the rudiments of hunting and taught him well.

Hardly a morning arrived when I didn't have to spend a good half an hour chasing small rodents or birds out of the kitchen before leaving for work.

But at least Theo was clean.

And, in a strange way, I envied the cats their ability to learn, change and grow.

I felt it was too late for me to be anything but the me I'd been moulded into. Max, however, had different ideas.

"You don't need me to fix that for you," Max said, as he looked under the car bonnet.

"I do," I insisted. "I'm hopeless with anything mechanical."

"You only say that because that's how you've been conditioned to think. Go and get your car manual. I'll go through it step by step with you while you do it."

I'd gone straight from school into marriage, then swiftly into motherhood.

There had never been a period of confidence building — but it was happening to me now!

"All right," I said. "But will you let me show you how to iron your shirts properly?"

He looked down at his crumpled shirt and grinned sheepishly. "I am a bit of a mess, aren't I?"

It was an understatement! I itched to get my hands on him, to trim his unruly hair, iron his shirts and press his jeans.

Yet, I'd been a perfect wife once and look where it had got me — any new man in my life would have to know how to look after himself. I felt my cheeks flush.

Suddenly, I'd gone from thinking of Max as the handyman, to thinking of him as the new man in my life!

OVER the next few months, I overcame my fear of heights and learned how to replace a broken roof tile.

It was the tip of a very big iceberg as, little by little, both my confidence and my abilities grew, until I was prepared to tackle anything.

I had never been truly independent in my life before and it seemed strange that now I owed my independence to another person.

I was so busy blossoming myself that, at first, I hardly noticed the change in Max. His small business grew, so that he had to take on extra help, and, with his enterprise blooming, so did his confidence.

By the end of the year, we were two different people.

Theo had grown, puzzlingly, into the most beautiful of cats.

I'd go so far as to say he was absolutely magnificent, and the lovely, dainty Desmond had learned to be a skilful hunter.

If Desmond had taught Theo how to improve his appearance, then Theo had taught Desmond how to take care of himself.

They had both found independence, but their lives were so closely intertwined that, as long as they were together, independence could go hang.

As it was with me and Max.

I loved being able to take care of myself and admired Max for being capable of the same.

But, when he kissed me that first time beneath the stars, my whole life shifted in perspective.

I heard the bells, saw the fireworks — and fell headlong into a bottomless well of love.

And, for the first time in my life, I knew the joy of being complete. ■

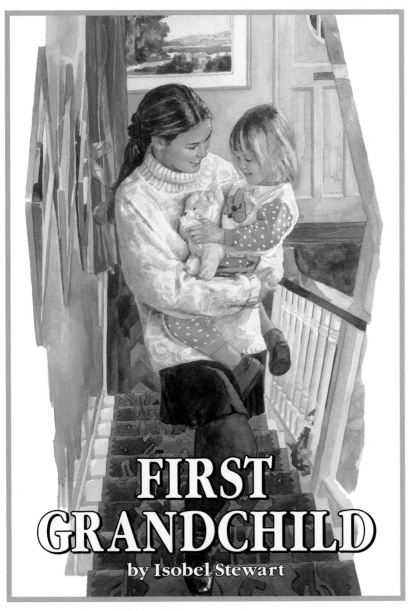

FIRST GRANDCHILD

by Isobel Stewart

She was so excited by the baby's birth, she forgot that little Mandy deserved her love just as much . . .

WAITING for the baby to be born, Janice sometimes thought, through the long months of her daughter-in-law's pregnancy, was a little like waiting for Christmas when she was a child — there was that same tingling excitement, that same breathless wonder.

She and her husband had always felt a little sad that Donald was an only child, and often, half-laughing, half-serious, Janice had said she'd just have to wait until she had grandchildren to spoil.

And now the waiting was almost over. Soon, she'd hold her grandchild in her arms. Her long-awaited first grandchild.

Because, of course, Mandy didn't count . . .

Oh, she was a nice little girl, and always very good when Donald and Beth brought her round to visit.

But it hadn't been easy, accepting that with Donald's marriage to Beth, he became an instant father. Janice had been sad for him, because he'd missed out on the early, carefree months of marriage, of being just the two of them, before children came along.

"He's old enough to know what he's doing, Jan," Tom had said quietly, when she'd once spoken about this. "He couldn't have found a nicer girl than Beth, and if he's happy to be a father to Mandy, then that should be enough for all of us."

That had been all — Tom wasn't a man for saying much — but she'd known that he meant it. And so she'd tried very hard to accept the little girl, to include her on every family occasion.

And, she thought, looking back over the two years of Donald and Beth's marriage, she hadn't done too badly.

She kept colouring-in books in the house for Mandy, and she'd knitted a jersey for her birthday, with Snoopy on it. She and Tom had gone with Donald and Beth to see Mandy in the Sunday School Nativity play, and they'd often babysat for her.

But at the end of it all, although she was fond of the little girl, she was still Beth's child. Donald's step-daughter.

Tom, now, seemed to find it easier. Whenever they visited,

he'd lift Mandy off her feet, and swing her round, asking, "And how's my best girl?"

Sometimes, when he did this, Janice would find Donald or Beth looking at her, a question in their eyes, or a plea for something more, something she wasn't able to give.

Even deciding what Mandy was to call them hadn't been easy.

"It had better be Tom and Janice, hadn't it?" Janice had suggested briskly.

No-one had argued, but Mandy didn't use the names too freely, and sometimes, to Tom's amusement, she'd say — for very soon she called Donald "Daddy" all the time — "Daddy's mummy", or "Daddy's daddy".

A WEEK before the baby was due, the phone rang soon after Tom had left for the office.

"Mum?" Donald's voice was strained.

"Mum, Beth's started — I'm just going to drive her to hospital, but Helen next door can't look after Mandy, because her kids have measles.

"Could I take Beth in, then bring Mandy round to you, so that I can go back to Beth?"

"Of course, Donald," Janice said immediately. "Lucky we're so near the hospital."

Mandy's eyes were very big in her small face when Donald brought her round, and she clung to his hand.

"Will I see Mummy soon, Daddy?" she asked, not quite steadily.

"Just as soon as the baby's born, poppet," he assured her. "Janice will bring you round to the hospital, and you'll be able to see Mummy and the baby."

He bent and kissed her, and then he kissed Janice.

When he'd gone, she looked down at Mandy, and realised that she felt more than a little dismayed at the thought of being left on her own with the child.

"Do you want your colouring books, Mandy?" she asked, but the little girl shook her head.

"I don't feel like colouring in, thank you," she said politely.

"Why don't we make some biscuits, then?" Janice suggested after a moment. "We could make the crunchy kind that —" for a moment she hesitated, but only for a moment "— that your daddy likes, then we can take some round to your mummy in hospital."

She found an apron, and tied it round Mandy's small middle.

"I look like a big lady, don't I?" Mandy asked, as Janice lifted her on to a kitchen stool, so that she could stir the butter and the sugar as they melted.

"Just like a big lady," Janice agreed.

They mixed the ingredients together, set the biscuits out on a tray, and then put the tray in the oven.

"Could we phone Tom and tell him we're getting our baby soon?" Mandy asked.

"That's a good idea," Janice replied, pretending to be surprised, for she'd been about to call Tom anyway. "Now why didn't I think of that?"

She dialled Tom's number, and handed the phone to Mandy.

"Tom, Janice and me are going to the hospital as soon as our baby's born, an' we made crunchy biscuits, an' I had on a big apron," Mandy said, all in one breath.

Smiling, Janice took the phone from her, gave Tom more details, and promised to call back as soon as there was any news.

She put the phone down, and looked at Mandy. What now?

"I feel like my colouring book now," Mandy said, and with considerable relief, Janice got the books and the crayons out.

From the kitchen, where she was preparing some vegetables for dinner, she watched the little girl.

Mandy's fair hair had fallen over her face, but Janice could see the tip of her small pink tongue sticking out of the corner of her mouth, and her head was tilted just to one side as she concentrated.

And, looking at her, a faint, elusive memory drifted into Janice's mind. The memory of another child, colouring in with just the same intensity, just the same tilt of the head.

SUDDENLY her hands stopped peeling the potatoes. It was Donald she was remembering, Donald who had looked like that. Donald — who wasn't this child's natural father.

Oh, there was no real likeness, but — just in that moment, Mandy had looked like Donald.

I'm just being foolish and fanciful, Janice told herself, but somehow the thought wouldn't go away.

Later, she spread some peanut butter on toast for Mandy's lunch.

"Is that how you like it?" she asked.

"Yes, thank you, but could you cut it into soldiers now?" Mandy answered.

"I used to do that for — your daddy," Janice said, after a moment.

"I know," Mandy replied. "That's why we do it."

Janice watched Mandy solemnly eating her soldiers, and felt a strange, disturbing warmth around her heart, as the little boy of all those years ago, and this little girl of today, somehow became linked.

After lunch, Mandy did some more colouring in, and Janice put her feet up and tried to concentrate on a magazine.

"Will the baby be my real brother or sister?" Mandy asked suddenly, taking her by surprise.

"Just as real as you want it to be, Mandy," she said, after a moment. "I'm pretty sure you won't ever think it's anything but real. And the baby will be very lucky, having a big sister like you."

Mandy looked at Janice, and once again the tilt of her head was Donald's.

"Will the baby call you Tom and Janice, too?"

Janice was taken aback. How did she answer that?

For a moment she was speechless, then suddenly the words were there.

"Well, Tom and I were wondering about that . . . would you like to call us Granny and Grandad? Then the baby could do the same . . ."

Mandy's small face flushed a deep rose-pink.

"I think I could," she said gravely.

The phone rang then, and Janice hurried to answer it. When she put it down, she turned to Mandy.

"You've got a little brother, Mandy," she said excitedly. "Let's get our coats, and we'll go round to the hospital."

BETH was sitting up in bed, flushed and pretty, and Janice kissed her and heard details of the baby's weight, and then Mandy told Beth and Donald about the biscuits she'd helped to make.

"We forgot to bring them," she realised suddenly.

"So we did," Janice agreed. "We'll bring them tomorrow. Come on, Mandy, let's have a look at the baby."

They eagerly crowded round the cradle at the side of Beth's bed, Mandy standing on tiptoe so she could see inside.

"Here he is," Donald said, carefully lifting out the tiny blue bundle.

Suddenly, laughter and love bubbled up inside Janice, because this miniature person was unbelievably like Tom.

"He's like your father," she said to Donald, gently touching a small hand.

"I know," Donald agreed, smiling, too. "Look, Mandy, here's your baby brother."

Janice looked again at the tiny red-faced baby.

"He's beautiful," she murmured. Janice turned to Beth, and almost bumped into a woman who was standing beside the next bed.

"Your first grandson?" the woman asked. "I'm here to see mine, too."

"Yes, my first grandson," Janice agreed. She took Mandy's small hand in hers. "But this is my granddaughter, Mandy."

And that was true, she thought with wonder. She was sorry it had taken her so long to realise just how true it was, but she was certainly going to make up for that now.

"Come on, Mandy, let's go home and phone Grandad," she said, "and we'll tell him all about the baby." ■

The Birdman And The Boy

by Margaret Waddingham

Both loners, they were soon to discover a common bond that forged a very special friendship.

THE boy squatted on his haunches like a small frog in front of the wooden cage. "Touch that bird and I'll box your ears!" Smith's bearded face was contorted into a frown as he materialised from amongst the trees.

The boy leaped up and spun round. "I wasn't doing nothing, mister, honest I wasn't. Just looking, that's all."

Smith pushed past him to the cage that was half hidden by a tangle of thorns and ivy. He peered inside at the bird and the bird stared back, unblinking, head slightly cocked.

Satisfied that no harm had been done, he turned on the boy again.

"You're not to come here," he said. "I won't have you frightening the creature."

"I was only looking," the boy said sulkily. "What you doing with him

72

anyway?" He pointed to the bandages on the bird's wing. "An' what's he got all that stuff wrapped round him for?"

Smith's left eyebrow lifted slightly. "I put it there for decoration," he said sarcastically.

"What's he want decorating for?"

"It's a she — and she's having a birthday."

The boy scowled. "Get away. You're having us on."

"Oh, am I?" the man said. "Well, laddie, I'll tell you what I'm not having you on about. I don't want you here. You were frightening the bird, staring at her like that.

"Now scat, and if I see you round here again, I'll put you in a cage!"

The boy stuck his bottom lip out defiantly. "It's not your wood," he said. "I can come here if I want!"

Smith surveyed him for a moment, then, holding out his arms so that the tattered leather fringes of his jacket fluttered like the wings of a great crow, he lunged towards him.

The boy took off and didn't stop running until he was out of the wood and back on to the track that led to his home.

A few days later, Smith came through the trees into the clearing carrying a small, dead rabbit by its hind legs.

Seeing the boy once more by the cage, he stopped short. "What you doing here? I thought I told you to stay away," he growled.

The boy ignored the question. "What you doing with this eagle, mister?"

"That's no eagle."

"What is it then?"

Smith crouched down beside the boy and looked at his bird. *"Buteo buteo,"* he said softly. "A buzzard to you."

"Cor!" the boy said. "He don't half look like an eagle. I seen pictures of them at school."

"No, she don't. Eagles are bigger, much bigger." Smith stood up again. "Now get out of my way," he said. "It's feeding time."

He opened the cage and threw in the small, limp body. The boy looked on with interest.

"Is that all she eats — just rabbits?" he asked

"No."

"What else then?"

"Any sort of carrion."

"What's carrion?"

"You ask too many questions, boy. And come away from her cage. She's not going to eat while we're standing over her."

They moved back to a respectful distance. "What's carrion?" the boy persisted.

"Dead things," Smith said.

"Cor!" the boy said. "How do you get things like that for her?"

"I just get them."

"Yes, but how?"

"I just get them, all right?"

The boy was silent for a moment, then he gazed up at Smith with big dark eyes, his straight hair flopping over his forehead.

"Where'd you get the bird?"

"Out there." Smith jerked his head. "On the high moor."

"What d'you call her?"

"I don't call her anything. I won't know her that long. You only give names to things if you're going to know them for a long time."

The boy considered the logic of the man's reasoning for a bit. "What's your name then?" he said at last.

"What's it to you?"

"I want to know what to call you."

"You've no cause to go calling me anything."

"You've got a name in the village," the boy persisted.

Between Smith's moustache and beard, there was a small movement that might have been a smile. "What do they call me?"

"They call you 'the car-man'."

"The car-man, eh? And what else do they say about me?"

The boy hesitated. "They say you're a bit daft."

"A bit daft?"

"They say that anyone who lives in a car in the middle of a wood must be a bit daft."

"Do you think I'm a bit daft?"

The boy shrugged. "I dunno," he said.

The man leaned forward, hands on knees, face close to the child's.

"Well, now listen here, laddie," he said quietly. "I am a bit daft and you should know that and not come back here again.

"Your ma wouldn't like it if she knew you were talking to me."

"Ain't got a ma."

"No ma?" Smith straightened up, thrown by the revelation.

"No. Never had one. I've always lived with me gran."

"All right, then, your gran wouldn't like it."

"She wouldn't mind, not if she knew you." He hesitated. "You're my friend."

Smith scowled. "I'm not your friend, I hardly know you. Go and play with mates of your own age."

"Ain't got none."

Smith stared at the boy in exasperation then turned abruptly and started through the trees in the direction of his car.

The boy stubbed the ground with his grubby trainers. "Hey, mister," he shouted after the retreating figure. "Can I see inside your car?"

Smith spun round angrily. "No you can't," he shouted. "It's private. Now get off with you and don't come back."

He turned away once more, calling over his shoulder, "And if I see you again, I will put you in that cage . . ."

I N the clearing opposite the cage, Smith was building an aviary. It was a large construction, solid at one end to give some protection from the weather, the remainder consisting of ash poles and wire netting.

The netting and boards he had obtained free from a nearby farmer in return for dismantling some unwanted hen-houses, and the ash poles he had felled himself.

Smith whistled tunelessly as he put the finishing touches to his work, pausing occasionally to drink strong, cold tea from a bottle.

The boy arrived and stood silently at a distance until eventually his curiosity overcame him and he called out, "What're you doing, mister?"

Smith straightened up and stroked his moustache pensively. "I thought I told you not to come back."

The boy looked rebellious. "I only want to know what you're making."

"You're too nosey by half," Smith observed. "And shouldn't you be at school?"

"Didn't want to go," the boy said.

"Didn't want to go? And what will your gran say about that when she finds out?"

"She won't. She's too busy on the farm. I don't like school."

He touched an ash pole and stuck his fingers through the wire netting. "What's this for?"

"It's an aviary."

"What's an aviary?"

Smith clicked his tongue in disgust. "You don't know anything, do you? If you went to school a bit, they'd teach you things like that. An aviary's a bird house."

"What do you mean by that?"

"Don't you ever stop asking questions?" Smith mopped his forehead in exasperation. "If I tell you, will you go away and not come back?"

The boy nodded, and Smith pointed to the cage.

"The buzzard's almost better," he said. "Before I let her go, I've got to get her into something bigger — like this aviary — so's she can flap her wings and get them strong again.

"When she's ready, I'll take her back to where I found her. And that," he said firmly, unscrewing his bottle and taking a mouthful of tea, "is all I've got to say on the subject."

The boy was not so easily put off. "You said the bandages were there as decoration 'cause it was her birthday."

"So it was."

"Get on. You'll be telling us there are fairies next."

"How old are you?"

"Ten."

"You're cheeky for ten. Hasn't anyone ever told you to mind your manners with your elders?"

The boy grinned. "Gran does. She cuffs me round the ear."

"I'll cuff you round the ear if you're cocky with me again."

"Well, why don't you tell me what's wrong with her?"

"Her wing was broken," Smith said.

"And now it's mended?"

He nodded, then said, "You're holding me up — now push off back home if you're not going to school."

"Did you mend it?" the boy asked.

"Me and nature together."

"Cor!" the boy said admiringly.

Smith, some staples clenched between his teeth, silently tapped down some more wire.

"Can't I help?" the boy wheedled.

"No," Smith said through his teeth. "I get on better on my own.

"Besides," he added, "we had an agreement. I tell you what I'm doing and why, and you go away and don't bother me again."

He dropped a staple. The boy darted forward, scrabbled about in the grass and handed it to him, but made no effort to leave.

Smith sighed heavily and handed him the remainder of the staples. "Here, " he said, defeated. "Pass these to me when I tell you to."

By late afternoon, the aviary was complete. A tree stump and stacked logs were placed in the sheltered end and branches were dug into the ground to look like trees at the other.

Boughs of evergreen were woven into the netting along one side.

They stood together and admired it. "Can we put her in now?" the boy asked.

"Tomorrow," Smith said firmly, and he started to collect his tools. "Here," he said suddenly, "you said your gran doesn't know you're off school."

The boy shook his head.

"You've got to promise me something before you come back again," Smith said. "And promise it proper this time. You've got to tell your gran that you're coming into the wood to see me — understand?"

"Why?"

"Because," Smith said patiently, "I'm a stranger and kids shouldn't talk to strangers. Your gran might not like it."

"You're not a stranger — you're my friend." The boy's eyes, huge and innocent, stared across at Smith.

Disconcerted, he shook his head. "I don't have friends," he muttered and picked up his tools.

"Besides, I'm the car-man. People think I'm daft."

"But you're not!"

"Your gran might think so."

"She won't."

"Tell her," Smith persisted, "or don't come back!"

The boy stuck his bottom lip out. "All right then."

"Promise? On your honour?"

The boy sighed truculently. "I promise on my honour. I'll tell her."

"Mind you do then."

Smith nodded curtly in his direction, tucked his tools under his arm and disappeared in the direction of his car without looking back.

SMITH waited all the following day for the boy, but he didn't turn up. At the end of the afternoon, he studied the buzzard and then decided to leave her where she was until the following morning, when he transferred her carefully into the aviary.

For the next three days, Smith watched and waited for the quick, darting movements through the trees that would herald the boy's arrival, and found to his surprise that he felt a keen sense of disappointment when he didn't come.

So, he thought, he'd told his gran and she'd forbidden him to come.

Early in the morning of the fourth day, however, the boy arrived in the clearing, his face pink with excitement.

"You're to meet my gran," he announced breathlessly.

"Who says?"

"Gran says. She says you're to come back to the farm this afternoon when I get home from school and have a cup of tea with us."

"And suppose I don't want to?"

The boy looked surprised, as though such a thought had never crossed his mind.

"Aw, go on, mister. Say you'll come."

Smith turned his back on the boy and stared into the aviary. Not long now, he thought, and the buzzard would be free — then he'd be alone again.

"You'll come, won't you?" The boy stood beside him tugging at the fringes of his jacket.

Smith shook him off. "All right, all right," he mumbled. "I'll come. But only for five minutes, mind. I don't hold with socialising."

Down a long, narrow track where bracken threatened to over-run heather, and farmland had been gouged out from the rock-strewn hillside, Smith found the farm where the boy lived with his gran.

She was a tall, severe-looking woman with large, work-roughened hands, a weather-beaten face and huge dark eyes like her grandson's.

She's about my age, Smith thought, surprised. He'd expected a grandmother to be much older.

Smith was grateful that the tea was a no-nonsense affair, just steaming char in big mugs and thick chunks of bread spread with peanut butter.

"The boy likes it," she said simply.

He nodded. "I like it, too. I'd forgotten."

Smith drank his tea and looked round the plain little kitchen. A tap dripped and a cupboard door swung open, the latch broken.

"I don't have time for the extras," she said defensively. "There's too much to do on my own."

She nodded in the direction of her grandson. "He does what he can." She smiled at the boy and he grinned back, spreading his freckles.

"I'll come tomorrow," he said as Smith left.

"After school, mind," the man warned.

"School's over — it's the weekend."

Smith's beard twitched and he walked out of the door, down the track and into the wood, back towards his car.

THE boy came each day, sometimes twice, and man and buzzard grew used to his presence. Soon he was allowed inside the aviary to feed her and he would stay inside, watching her eat, admiring her brown and cream plumage.

When she flew round the aviary, he laughed with delight and even Smith would allow himself to feel a little glow of satisfaction.

Then, one day, from somewhere above the treetops, there came the sound of another buzzard's cry.

The grounded bird stood still for a moment, head to one side, listening, then suddenly she flew round and round her cage and the air was filled with a haunting meeiou, meeiou.

Smith nodded skywards. "That'll be her mate, I reckon. It won't be long now."

"What won't?"

"Letting her go."

"When? Tomorrow?"

"Maybe," the man said. "Depends on the wind. You've got to have the right thermals."

"What's thermals?"

And Smith grumbled at the boy for his ignorance and the boy said anxiously that Smith mustn't let her go until he was there, too.

Smith grumbled again, but he didn't say no . . .

The buzzard crouched low on a soft cushion of crumpled newspaper at the bottom of the box as Smith and the boy carried her to the high moor.

"Look up there,"Smith said suddenly, pointing to a small dot lazily sailing high overhead. "Reckon that's her mate."

Carefully he opened the box and lifted out the bird. Sadly the boy ran his finger down her back for the last time, until Smith released her and, with a heavy beat of wings, she was gone.

She rose up and up, calling to her mate, and from above her there came an answering cry.

Then, high above the man and the boy, as though performing an elegant dance of farewell, the two birds hovered together.

For breathless minutes, the watchers gazed upwards, until at last, with a final sweeping circle, the birds turned and flew away.

The boy stared skywards for a long time after they were gone. Then he rubbed fiercely at his eyes with the back of his hands and a small, sad noise escaped from his throat.

Smith put a hand on the thin shoulders and squeezed gently. "Reckon we'll go and make some tea now, laddie," he said.

"We never gave her a name. We must have known her long enough to give her a name."

Smith considered. "All right then — how about Beauty. Beauty Buteo."

"Beauty Buteo," the boy repeated thoughtfully. "She'd have liked that."

Smith stooped to pick up the empty box. "Here," he said, "catch hold of the other end of this."

The boy did so, and together they went off down the hill.

"I suppose you don't want me to come again," the boy said in a small voice. "Not now you haven't got Beauty any more."

"I've been thinking," Smith said. "Maybe your gran would like me to do a few odd jobs round the place for her. I wouldn't want paying — I'd do them as a friend."

The boy looked suspicious. "Whose friend?" he asked.

"Yours, of course!"

"'Spect she'd like that." The boy looked relieved.

Smith strode on down the hill and the boy walked beside him, now and then running an extra step to keep up.

Shyly Smith glanced sideways at him as they walked.

"You can call me Smith if you want," he said. "Now what do I call you?"

And somewhere between his moustache and beard there was a small movement.

It could even have been a smile . . . ◼

She was so homesick, he began to wonder if her longing for England was stronger than her love for him . . .

Your Dream Of Home

Marian Hipwell

PAUL stood on the patio and watched Ellen shading her eyes as she looked up at the aircraft droning overhead. He'd noticed her doing that a lot recently.

As if aware of his eyes on her, she turned and smiled quickly at him.

"It looks so beautiful, I can't help wondering where it's going . . ."

He knew what was in her mind. It could be going home. And I could be on it.

His face shadowed. Home. So they'd come to nothing, all his hopes that Ellen would be able to settle here.

He turned and walked back into the cool of the house. Would she leave him? Would that wistful longing that she couldn't hide from him at times grow so strong that he couldn't hold on to her?

He could hear her hurrying after him, her eyes anxious.

"Paul, I'm sorry —"

"It's all right, honey. I understand."

Sometimes he wished he didn't understand. She loved him, he knew that.

But it was a love which hadn't yet been able to cushion her from the waves of homesickness which washed over her so heavily at times that it lay between them like the ocean which separated their two countries.

He'd expected her to miss her home, but never like this.

Sometimes he glimpsed the longing in her eyes, and was afraid she wouldn't be there when he looked round again — afraid she'd have flown away, like those beautiful birds who couldn't stand the harsh winters in their own land.

What was the answer? He'd asked himself that question so many times. Sell up and take her back to her own country and hope to get a job?

It would be worth it, he felt at times, just to see that look leave her eyes. Not that it was there all the time — only on days like today, when she was quiet and obviously thinking of home.

"I hoped —" He looked at her helplessly. "I know it's difficult for you, but I've done my best —"

"Of course you have." She touched his arm. "And I'm coping better now. I don't ask for biscuits any more in supermarkets and look surprised when they give me bread rolls."

She laughed, a self-conscious, constrained sound that didn't fool either of them. There was much more to this than the superficial difference in their lifestyles.

"If you want to go back for a visit . . ." He looked at her hesitantly, hoping she'd refuse, and was disappointed and unreasonably hurt when he saw the hope flicker in her eyes before she quenched it.

"You can't get the time off —"

"Not me. Just you. Go for a few weeks. Until —"

Until what? Until she no longer felt as if the heart had been ripped out of her when she left? Until this alien Californian coast somehow began to look like home to her?

"Try to understand, Paul." She spoke with quiet intensity. "I love you so much. But — I feel so strange here, at times."

"People will always help you here," he said, trying to stifle his impatience.

"I know. They're great people. And this is a great country. But —" she sighed, searching for words to make him understand "— it would be the same if this were Spain, or Holland, or —"

"I get your point." He turned away.

"How would you feel if it were you?" she asked desperately.

He'd already asked himself that question, in his attempts to understand.

How would it feel to live somewhere else, far away from this sunny place where outdoors met indoors with a scarcely definable line?

It was the essence of the place he would miss, he realised, the streets which looked and smelled familiar, the people who spoke with the same accent as he did. Home. His home. But not hers.

"Did you really mean it about going back — to Britain — for a week or two?" She'd been going to say going home, he knew it as well as she did. And again, he was hurt by the way she'd seized on his suggestion so eagerly.

"Sure. Take all the time you want." He'd been about to say all the time you need, but that might be a very long time . . .

He saw her off on an early flight a few days later. She'd been as excited as a child at the thought of going.

He'd tried not to spoil it for her, yet all he'd been conscious of was fear that she wouldn't come back, that she'd forget, in her happiness at being home, all that they had between them.

Yet what did they have between them, if she couldn't be happy living in the same place as him?

HE stood for a long time, lost in his own thoughts, after the aircraft carrying her had disappeared from sight.

It had been that Englishness of hers which had first attracted him to her; a gentle shyness which had captivated him. Yet the things which had first drawn him to her had become the stumbling blocks in the end.

She'd seemed so enthusiastic about a new life thousands of miles away from her home, and had seemed to settle down well in the beginning.

Yet, as time went on, he'd caught those wistful glances when she thought he wasn't looking. It wasn't that she didn't love him, it wasn't that simple.

Later, he wandered back to the house, wanting to be by himself where he could let his misery show.

Memories crowded in on him, fleeting recollections of their year together.

The day his family had come over, not long after he'd brought Ellen home to California. They'd had lunch on the patio, he recalled.

It had been an unusually overcast day, and he hadn't been surprised when light rain had begun to fall.

Among much good-natured grumbling, they'd all moved indoors. Nobody had minded, really. It had been a hot dry summer and the rain was welcome.

Chatting with his family, it had been some moments before he realised Ellen was still outside. When he'd gone to investigate, he'd found her standing on the patio, her face held up towards the rain. When he'd reached her side, he'd seen the wetness on her face and known it wasn't just raindrops.

"It's the first time," she'd said quietly. "The first time it's rained since I came."

"You've been doing a rain dance when I wasn't looking, haven't you?" Fear had made him treat the whole thing in a jokey way. "You're telling me you like the rain?"

It had been a few seconds before she'd answered his question.

"I miss the rain," she'd said. "I never thought I would, but I do."

He'd hated the rain, when he'd worked in England. Caught frequently in heavy showers, he'd sheltered, shivering, in shop doorways, thinking of home and the golden sun which clothed everything in its warm glow.

"That's why everything is so green," she'd said unexpectedly. "Because of the rain, you see. It has its compensations."

"One of them, I hope, isn't giving crazy people who stand out in it pneumonia!" He'd taken her arm and gently drawn her back into the house, among his family. Yet her glance had kept going to the window, he'd noticed, after that.

Had he tried to understand, really understand, he asked himself now? Had he remembered the wistful longing for his home which had swept over him at unexpected moments during his stay in England?

But he'd known he would go home eventually. For Ellen it was forever. And if he didn't want to lose her, he had to find some way of helping her come to terms with that.

Two days later, when he was rummaging for a shirt in the wardrobe, he came across a tissue-wrapped parcel. He'd seen it once before, he realised, when Ellen was unpacking after he'd brought her here.

"A garden gnome!" He'd looked at her in amusement. "Whatever will we do with that?"

How insensitive he must have sounded, he thought now. And how foolish he'd made her feel, for she'd taken the parcel from him and put it on the wardrobe shelf.

"I bought it a long time ago for our garden at home," she'd said quietly. "It was just a piece of home, that's all."

A piece of home. Now, taking the gnome from its wrappings, Paul stared at it. Was it possible to have an English garden in the middle of California — a place where Ellen could go, whenever she found reality hard to face up to? He didn't know, but he could try.

It took him a week or so to get it the way he wanted it. The plants were hard to find, but he managed to create a herbaceous border, just like the ones . he'd seen in English gardens.

He built an arbour and trained roses over it, and dug a small pond in one corner. Finally, right next to the patio, where Ellen would be able to see it as soon as she came back, he placed the gnome.

THREE days after he'd finished, the telephone rang. It was Ellen, telling him she was at the airport.

"Ellen!" He could hardly believe it. "I didn't expect you to —"

"It was a last-minute booking. I decided to come back early . . ."

"I'll come for you," he promised. "I'm on my way to the airport."

The look had gone from her eyes, he saw, as she walked towards him, that wistfulness that had haunted him. But for how long? Even as he hugged her, he was wondering that. How long before she wanted to leave him again?

And then they were both talking at once, each trying to tell the other how much they'd missed them.

"Did it rain while you were there?" he asked, as they drove away from the airport.

"All the time," she told him. "So much so that even I'd had enough of it." There was a lightness in her tone which reassured him.

When they were inside the house, he drew her into his arms.

"I've missed you," he said quietly. "Come and see what's been keeping me so busy while you were away."

He led her into the living-room, towards the window. She made no response for a few moments and he was afraid again, afraid he'd made a mistake.

His clumsy attempts at trying to merge her old life with her new life had only made things worse. When he looked at her, he saw that there were tears in her eyes.

"It's lovely," she said at last. She pointed towards the gnome. "And isn't that —"

"The little guy you brought from home — yes," he told her. "It was time we found him a place."

Opening the patio doors, Ellen stepped outside. Paul let her wander around for a while, looking at everything, before he joined her.

"I'm sorry there's no rain," he said gently. "But there will be. We're not really all that different, you know."

"I know." She hesitated. "I've been feeling as if we were standing on the opposite sides of a gulf," she explained. "We both needed to take a step towards each other, Paul. This is yours."

"And yours?" He looked searchingly into her eyes. "Did you manage it — or was the jump too wide for you?"

She frowned, as if not quite sure herself.

"All I can say is that one day, back in England, I looked up at a passing plane and I thought, that plane could be on its way to Paul. And if so, I could be on it . . ."

His arm tightened around her. So she was beginning, slowly and tentatively, to put down roots.

She'd go home again, he knew. But each time she would return sooner. And one day, she'd be able to look beyond that little garden he'd made for her and see just what she had in her own backyard.

"Welcome home," he said softly. ■

ANIMAL MAGIC

by Audrey E. Groom

She'd given the animals a home — not realising they had something even more precious to offer in return.

TO my friend, Irma —"The solicitor gave a discreet little cough and raised his eyes momentarily from the will.

He let them run over the assembled family and friends of the late Charlotte Finch.

Irma wasn't expecting anything. After all, Charlotte had quite a large family.

Nevertheless, she had been asked to come and now she would be glad if the solicitor would stop play-acting and just get on with it!

Her well-manicured fingers gripped her neat leather handbag.

"To my friend, Irma, I leave —" yet another pause "— ten thousand pounds."

An undisguised gasp ran around the table and the colour drained from Irma's face. This was unbelievable.

She and Charlotte had been friends since school — and Charlotte was pretty well off, but ten thousand pounds!

Her mouth felt dry. Someone pushed a glass of water towards her.
The solicitor was speaking again. What was he saying now?

"Attached to the last bequest there is a proviso, a condition."

The solicitor looked all around him again, enjoying the curiosity on every face.

"A proviso," he continued, "and it is, in Mrs Finch's own words, 'that my friend, Irma, shall take my dog, Fred, and my cat, Dulcie. And that she shall care for them, in the state to which they are accustomed, for the rest of their natural lives'."

There was another gasp and then silence.

Irma drained the glass of water this time, for she had never owned an animal in her life!

Feeling hot and confused, she asked to be excused from listening further and, moving quickly from the table, left the room and went to the bathroom and rinsed her face.

SHE had been shocked by the amount of money, albeit pleasantly, and shocked by the animals — but in the opposite way.

A dog and a cat! Charlotte's home had been full of pets and children, noise and muddle.

But Irma's solitary household was like herself — quiet, immaculate and tidy.

So why had Charlotte done this? Well, Irma thought, she could take a guess at that.

Apart from the practical reasons, that Charlotte's children were at different universities around the country, it was her friend's way, even from the grave, of trying to introduce her to a different lifestyle.

"You're missing so much, Irma, by not having animals in your life," Charlotte had often said to her. "They give such affection, joy and companionship."

Charlotte had always been in love with life, making it all the more tragic that she'd died so young.

Irma had been very fond of Charlotte, very fond indeed, but, she thought now, that didn't mean she wanted to live the same way as her late friend.
The mere idea!

True, she sometimes felt a little lonely, but life was much tidier lived alone, with few problems or responsibilities.

Well, she wasn't going to be alone now, was she?

What Charlotte couldn't do in life, it looked as though she had managed in death. Unless Irma refused the bequest!

But she couldn't do that.

Even if there hadn't been any money involved, she couldn't turn down a friend's last wish, could she?

That's what Charlotte had been banking on, of course!

It was a sobering thought and she felt the need to talk it over with someone. So she went home and phoned Douglas.

Irma had no great opinion of the opposite sex. They seemed to her, on the whole, vain, untidy, and incapable of serious, unselfish thought.

Women were so much more logical, so much more practical, she truly believed.

However, she considered Douglas the exception that proved the rule.

THEY had been friends for a few years now — friends in the strictly platonic sense, of course — as they both attended the same church.

"Douglas," she begged him now on the phone, "please come over right away."

His car drew up on the driveway 15 minutes later and Irma had her front door open even before he reached it. He looked concerned.

"Irma, what's wrong?"

Douglas followed Irma into her lounge.

He wasn't good-looking but his face was interesting, with lively blue eyes, an enigmatic smile and the look of knowing more than the next man.

They sat down and Irma poured out the details of the will. "And what am I supposed to do, Douglas?" she asked at last. "Ten thousand pounds will pay for my new roof.

"But, a dog and cat! The dog sheds hair all over the place and —" she hesitated, "— the cat has a . . . litter tray in the kitchen!"

Douglas's enigmatic smile widened.

"Douglas, don't laugh!" Irma burst out earnestly. "It's not funny.

"I can't refuse anyway, can I? She was my best friend. Even without the ten thousand, it would be difficult to refuse her last wish."

"And with it, it's impossible!" Douglas said, his eyes twinkling.

CHARLOTTE'S neighbour, Jean, brought the animals round a couple of days later. A big Golden Retriever-cross and a green-eyed black cat.

She unloaded their beds and blankets from her small car and put them in the hall.

"There's plenty of food for them for a week or so, and here are their vet's cards and Fred's lead.

"They're good animals, Irma, you won't find them any trouble."

As the car pulled away, Irma looked at the big dog sitting on her smooth, beige-coloured carpet and saw there was a scattering of hairs already.

And where was Dulcie? Oh, no!

Dulcie was in the lounge, clawing at the settee!

Panicking, she put a hand on the telephone. But, no, it was no use. She couldn't call Douglas every five minutes!

She took a deep breath and strode through to the kitchen.

She supposed she'd have to prepare them something to eat and then take Fred for a walk.

She had never walked a dog in her life and was a little embarrassed by Fred's attraction to trees.

In fact, she was quite glad when they reached the recreation ground and she could let him off the lead.

But she was even more embarrassed when he went chasing off after a little spaniel bitch and she had to go panting across the grass after him!

The woman with the spaniel was plump and round-faced, and smiled warmly at Irma.

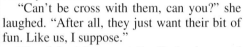

"Can't be cross with them, can you?" she laughed. "After all, they just want their bit of fun. Like us, I suppose."

Bit of fun! Irma put Fred's lead on and tramped back home with him.

When she got back, Dulcie was asleep in the middle of her bed, curled up very warmly.

And there was still that revolting litter tray to arrange for her in the kitchen, Irma mused.

She vacuumed the hall twice before she sat down to watch television, but she couldn't get rid of the dog hair.

And it gradually dawned on Irma, too, that Fred and Dulcie seemed to have some sort of arrangement by which one wanted to go out as the other came in.

She spent all the evening opening and shutting doors for them.

She was exhausted by the time she went to bed. So was Fred, sleeping underneath it and Dulcie, snoozing at the foot of it.

But there was worse to come.

Next day, the lady next door brought in some bones for Fred.

Irma shuddered when she found him gnawing them later on her nice lounge carpet and had to sit down in the kitchen with a strong cup of tea.

S HE needed lots of very strong cups of tea over the next few days. Muddy footmarks, a dead mouse at the back door, a pot-plant broken, were just a few of the trials Irma faced.

Then there was the patch of perfect lawn Fred had dug up in order to bury his precious bone.

The final straw, though, was definitely Dulcie being sick in the bathroom.

Take them back, all Irma's instincts screamed. Take the animals back. Tell them you don't want the money, either — friendship has its limits!

But, even as the reached for the lead and cat-basket, she saw in her imagination Charlotte's gentle and trusting face.

And she knew that every time she thought of her friend in the future, she would feel guilty if she let her down like this.

It was no good. She'd have to try again — with new rules.

For a start, she'd confine greasy bones to the kitchen by always remembering to shut doors.

She'd make sure Dulcie didn't overeat. And she'd thoroughly brush both animals every day — that should keep their hair-shedding down.

Irma was going to be very business-like about this whole procedure.

But what she didn't realise was that brushing animals brings you into close contact with them.

They purr to you, or lick your hand. So it was that Dulcie would push her head against Irma's hand, anxious to be stroked, and Fred would roll over with his feet in the air, asking to have his tummy rubbed.

Then, one very special day, running her hand through Fred's thick coat, Irma found herself asking softly, "Who's my lovely boy, Fred?"

Then, quite shaken by what she had said, she jumped up quickly, glad that no-one had heard her.

But he was lovely, wasn't he, she couldn't help thinking.

Then, dressed more sensibly, in an anorak and flat shoes, she began taking Fred for long walks.

The dog soon learned to come running back to her when she called, nuzzling his wet nose under her hand, wagging the whole back half of his body with pleasure at being close to her.

Gradually, too, Irma slipped into other new habits, like shopping for pet food, occasionally bathing Fred, and having Dulcie curled up on her lap when she was watching television.

Douglas began to call round more often, too, not waiting for an invitation as he'd always done in the past.

But, one day, he came round to find Irma very upset.

"It's Fred," she sniffed. "He won't eat any breakfast, he's got a dry hot nose and he whimpers when I stroke him."

"We'll take him along to the vet's," Douglas soothed.

IRMA had never in her life been to a vet's and was quickly fascinated, but also rather touched, by the customers in the surgery.

Like the old lady, hugging her equally-old little terrier and the little girl with her rabbit in a shawl.

Then there was the big rugby-playing type with two kittens in a basket, chatting sympathetically to a woman with a sick canary.

Fred lifted sad eyes to hers and she stroked him — and was amazed to realise that she understood how the others felt about their pets.

"Oh, I do hope he'll be all right," she said worriedly.

Douglas put his hand over hers. "He'll be all right, Irma," he said softly.

They went into the surgery together.

Up on the examination table, expert hands examined Fred.

Irma stood beside Douglas, while the vet looked at Fred's teeth and eyes and into his mouth.

She felt her own mouth dry with anxiety as she watched and she suddenly realised the truth.

She had grown to love that big, messy, hairy, troublesome creature! She couldn't bear it if anything happened to him now.

At last, the vet turned to them. He was smiling. "Just a tummy upset, I think. An injection and a course of tablets should do the trick. He'll probably be OK in a few days."

"Thank goodness!" Irma sighed with relief as they climbed back into Douglas's car.

"Thank goodness it's nothing much. And it was awfully nice of you to come with me, Douglas. It wasn't really your worry."

Douglas laughed. "Your worries are my worries, Irma."

How kind he was! She saw that now.

She'd always realised that he was an astute and intelligent man — head and shoulders above his fellow men.

But it was only now that she was beginning to appreciate his caring qualities and his natural, totally genuine warmth.

But she also realised something else — that she herself was perhaps less than caring in return.

She watched now as Douglas turned and patted Fred's brown head as he lay on the back seat.

"Actually," Irma said, then, "I didn't know how fond of animals you really are, Doug."

He smiled. "There's a lot of things you don't know about me, Irma!"

She thought about that remark once she got home and decided that, perhaps, there were really a lot of things she did know about him, but with which she hadn't concerned herself.

She'd never shown the slightest interest in his music collection, for instance.

Or offered to go with him to an art gallery, or to prepare his favourite meal even though she was quite a good cook — and he was anything but!

On Sunday, she asked him to lunch and made boeuf en croûte, followed by raspberry pavlova, his very favourite meal.

Douglas brought the wine. "Thank you, Irma," he said. "That was wonderful." And, shortly after, she noticed he'd fallen asleep on the settee with Dulcie on his lap.

Irma, sitting opposite him in the armchair, looked through the paper and saw that there was a Mozart recital at their local concert hall.

Douglas might like to hear that, she thought. And, next Sunday, perhaps they'd have rack of lamb, another of his favourites.

She closed her eyes, Fred snoozing at her feet.

And somewhere in heaven, Charlotte Finch smiled. ■

Sally's Keepsake

by Audrey E. Groom

All she wanted was something to remember Gran by. Yet, how to choose when everything in the cottage brought back memories?

SALLY looked out from her bedroom window. Such a perfect morning, fluffy white clouds, bright autumn sunshine, the garden tinged with russet and gold. She sighed. Too perfect a morning for the task which lay ahead of her and her mother. And yet it must be done . . .

Sally was home for her first weekend from college. Her much-loved grandmother had died a few weeks back. And now that the funeral was over and the will read, she and her mother must set about clearing Gran's cottage.

What memories a morning like this brought back of Gran, and her cottage. Planting seeds with her, gathering flowers, picking tomatoes and raspberries and strawberries, clearing paths, and building snowmen in the winter.

How Sally had adored her gran, and they'd been the best of friends . . . Today would somehow be more like saying goodbye than the funeral had been. Still, it had to be done.

"You should take something of your gran's away with you — something that will keep her close to you," said Sally's mum, as they emptied wardrobes and drawers.

Sally looked lovingly at Gran's clothes. She could just see her grandmother in that white silk blouse that she'd kept for special occasions . . . and there was the thick tweed skirt she'd worn when they went on long country rambles.

Each item of clothing they folded and placed on the pile brought back some memory of Gran to Sally. But there wasn't really anything there she wanted to keep.

There was even a pair of trousers! Gran had thought herself greatly daring when she wore those, but she'd said they were so comfortable for gardening.

When they moved to the second bedroom — the guest room — Sally even found herself laughing.

"Look, Mum," she said, "do you remember Gran buying these?"

Sally's mother smiled, too.

Gran had come across an old toy at a jumble sale — a sort of acrobat who walked on a rope between two sticks. And she'd become so fond of him that she had begun going to flea-markets and antique fairs to buy others like them.

Not that they were real antiques, or of great value, but Gran had enjoyed them, and so had her young visitors. There was a small collection of them here. But somehow Sally knew none of them was what she was looking for and so they, too, went into a box for the charity shop.

After the bedrooms, they moved downstairs to the living-room.

Here, of course, was more of the colourful tapestry of Gran's life.

There were vases and ornaments, framed photos and pictures, cushions, chair-backs and her special little foot-stool.

SALLY remembered as a child sitting on that for hours in front of the fire, her head against Gran's knee. Gran would either read from her favourite book, or tell her a story that she'd made up.

Sally had liked those stories best.

Gran had had such a vivid imagination! And yet there had always been a happy ending. Always a warm comfortable feeling to take home to bed with her, so that, no matter how topsy-turvy the world had seemed, she had felt sure that soon it would straighten out again.

Sally smiled. Gran's comfort had extended far beyond small childhood troubles.

Only a couple of years back, when Sally had been breaking her heart over a certain young man in the sixth form, Gran had provided a very sympathetic shoulder to cry on.

No, none of the things she'd seen so far painted quite the right picture of Gran.

"Let's have a cup of tea, shall we, Mum?" Sally suggested.

While waiting for the tea to brew, Sally looked again round the kitchen of the cottage — perhaps the most familiar room of all.

And there, lying on the dresser, she saw it. The old well-worn book. Gran's old cookery book! She brought it to the table.

As they comforted themselves with hot strong tea, Sally and her mother turned the pages.

On the first pages there were recipes in a childish hand all spelt wrongly. "My favorit pudding", "Sirrup Tart".

Then there were recipes cut from newspapers and old magazines with Gran's comments at the side. *This was good,* and much later, *Ben liked this.*

Ben, of course, was Grandad's name.

Later came drop-scones and soda-bread, flapjacks and steamed puddings, and everyday fruit cake.

Presumably there were hard times when Gran had a family to feed. *Cheap to make*, she'd written against some recipes, or, *Makes a lot.*

But then there were the others labelled, *For special occasions* — rich flans and trifles, and light cream sponges.

Perhaps the most poignant was towards the end. *This is Sally's favourite,* Gran had written, and Sally wiped her eyes as a stray tear ran down her cheek.

But looking up at her mother she smiled again.

"This is what I want, Mum. This will be my keepsake. This is Gran and her whole life, isn't it?"

Later, as they walked home, Sally reflected that, after all, the day hadn't proved too unhappy.

And sitting on her bed that night and looking again at the recipe book, she reflected, I suppose it was because you were helping us, Gran.

She closed the book and held it closely to her.

"I believe you always will," she said softly. ■

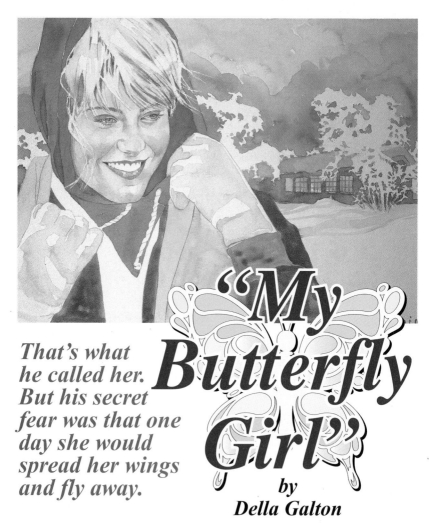

"My Butterfly Girl"

That's what he called her. But his secret fear was that one day she would spread her wings and fly away.

by
Della Galton

"I LOVE you, Stella . . ." Michael knew at once that it was the wrong thing to say. The phrase hung in the air like an accusation, somehow implying that she was responsible, and he knew that wasn't true.

She was just so easy to love.

Now he studied her face, her eyes bright and blue, staring away from him into the peach and grey horizon.

The afternoon sun was low in the sky and the rising hills cast long shadows over the valley floor.

Stella still had her hand in his, and Michael was frightened to move in case she found an excuse to pull it away.

"Let's walk for a while," she said at last, turning so that her blonde hair

94

fanned out gently in the cold breeze. "It's too good an afternoon to waste."

Too good an afternoon, too good a life, Michael thought, as he fell into step beside her. He'd been crazy to say anything about love, crazy to jeopardise the easy relationship they shared.

He would have kept quiet if he could have borne it, but the pressure of wanting to tell her had built up until he could resist it no longer.

He glanced at her as they walked. She was so slim and lovely and perfect. His butterfly girl, he secretly called her. She was like a butterfly landing fleetingly on the brightest of flowers, before skimming on to the next.

And that was where the problem lay. There were far brighter flowers than him.

His feet were firmly planted on the land they walked across, his strong fingers used to tending to the hundreds of manual jobs about his parents' farm.

Michael knew she hadn't fallen for his looks. He'd never kidded himself that he was attractive.

"Strong and sturdy," his mother always said. "Like Ben, the reliable old cart-horse." No, Michael had simply been there at the right time.

He'd found Stella outside the local disco one November night, six weeks ago, crying as if her heart might break.

He hadn't said much, just being there had seemed to be enough, and it had seemed enough ever since — at least, he'd thought so.

His parents had warned him off from the start.

"It'll never last, girls like that don't go for the likes of you," his mother had said, her hands white with flour, her sharp brown eyes not looking at him, but kneading the bread more aggressively as she spoke.

"Careful, lad — she's on the rebound." He remembered his father's advice, gruff and matter-of-fact as he knocked his pipe ash into the ashtray.

He'd tried to heed their advice, as he always had, but somehow this time his head just didn't want to know.

All he knew was that she seemed to need him, and when she looked up at him with those wide, bluebell eyes, how could he do anything else but be there for her?

She seemed comfortable in his arms, and he loved to hold her, but he never tried to take it further.

They would walk around the village and across his father's fields, hand in hand. When he took her home at night she'd proffer her face to be kissed like a little girl and he would allow his lips to brush her forehead in a big-brotherly fashion.

But that was all.

Deep inside there was a part of him that was more afraid of losing her than he dared to admit.

THEY'D walked a long way before she spoke, her voice soft, her eyes still fixed on the darkening sky. "We found out that Amber's in foal today," she said.

"That's good." Michael knew he sounded awkward and stilted and that there was nothing he could do about it.

Perhaps she would just ignore the words he wished he'd never said. She was like that sometimes. She seemed to see only the good things in life, and when something bad happened she was invariably looking the other way.

But, as they reached the big chestnut tree at the border of his father's land, she drew him to a halt.

"I heard what you said earlier, Michael."

His heart thudded painfully and he didn't meet her eyes.

"I've always known," she continued. "Your love is like a big, warm, comfy coat that I can wrap myself up in when I'm cold."

He risked a look at her eyes and saw a mixture of sadness and amusement and just a hint of something else.

Perhaps it was the thought of making a decision that she knew would hurt him.

"I wouldn't have survived without you," she said quietly. "When Timmy went, I was quite sure my life was finished."

"And now you've found out it's just beginning . . ."

She nodded. "Yes I have, but I could never have done it without you."

"You'd have coped." His voice was gruff and he could no longer look at her. He had spent all of Christmas thinking about Stella, dreaming of starting a new year — a new life — together.

He had hoped against hope that his butterfly girl would come to earth, only now it seemed she was all set to spread her wings once more.

Already he could feel pain tightening his breathing and making it difficult to speak. The moment he'd dreaded all these weeks was finally here. She didn't need him any more.

She'd tried to tell him earlier but he hadn't let her. He'd interrupted with his foolish declarations of love.

"Timmy's back," she was saying. "I bumped into him in the Post Office yesterday."

"He's finished doing the educated bit at college then, has he?" Michael hoped she wouldn't hear the bitterness that he was trying so desperately to hide, but he wasn't superhuman.

"Yes, he's here for good now."

The words smothered Michael's hopes like a wet cloth. Would she go back to Timmy, he wondered. Would he have to see the two of them about the village, starry-eyed with wedding plans, as the gossips wagged "I-told you-so" fingers?

"Anyway, it's time we were getting back." Michael slipped his hand from hers and strode ahead of her down the slope towards the farm.

He didn't need to look back to know she was following. He could hear her butterfly steps hurrying to catch up.

But there was no reason for her to catch up now, was there? Not now Timmy was back with his slick, dark hair and arrogant smile.

And it was then that Michael noticed there was an unfamiliar heaviness about her footsteps. He wanted to find out why and he paused to wait for her.

I'M cold, Michael." She was breathing heavily as she reached him. He sighed and slipped his jacket from his shoulders. Well, that was easy and perhaps it was the last thing he would ever do for her.

"Not that sort of cold, Michael . . ."

He looked at her, uncomprehending, as she let his proffered jacket fall to the ground.

"Do you remember that I said your love was like a comfy, warm coat that I can wrap myself up in when I'm cold?"

Michael nodded. "Well," she went on, "I want to wear that coat . . . always." Stella rested her head on his chest.

"What about Timmy?" he asked feebly, but suddenly he knew the answer even before she spoke.

"Timmy is a very handsome man, Michael, a real charmer — but he hurt me a lot, and he never cared about me the way you do."

She looked up at him, and he could see the truth of her words reflected in her eyes. "I suppose I've loved you since that night you found me crying my eyes out on the disco steps, but I told myself that it couldn't really be love, not so soon after Timmy.

"I thought I must be on the rebound."

Her eyes sparkled. "Then, when I met him yesterday, I realised that I was wrong. Bitterness about Timmy hadn't clouded my feelings — I love you, Michael. I really do."

A warm red glow, like that of the sun now sinking below the horizon, spread through Michael from head to toe.

Very gently, he cupped her face in his rough, work-worn hands and, with the last of the evening's rays stretching soft fingers of romance across the sky, he kissed her tenderly, in an extremely un-brotherly fashion, for the very first time . . . ■

The days of the year go by so fast
With time like a flowing river.
Before we know it, the present is past,
Summer warmth turned to winter
shiver.

Your familiar voice on the telephone
Is comforting; I'm no longer alone.
We talk and laugh as we remember
Days that we shared,
like that day last September.

We walked together down the lane,
Enjoying the sunshine after rain.
Stone-built walls, and a five-barred gate.
A leaning tree. We rest and wait.

Out of nowhere comes an amazing sight
A snorting pig is running in fright.
He races past us, fear in his eyes.
Then comes his hunter. What a surprise.

You roar with laughter as I recall
The duck that chased him along the wall.
Her wings were raised, her eyes flashed fire.
What had he done to raise her ire?

Had he eaten her eggs, or trampled her nest?
Or merely disturbed her noonday rest?
The memory lingers. It's so absurd
To think of a pig being chased by a bird.

Your phone call tells me that you care.
I love the memories we share.
Though we are often far apart
You've always a place within my heart.

Shared Memories

A poem by Joyce
Stranger, inspired by
an illustration
by Mark Viney.

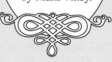

Husband On Call!

by Teresa Ashby

Couldn't he see that it wasn't his medical expertise she needed now, but simply his love and support?

S ARA couldn't be sure if it was the ringing of the telephone which woke her, or Ben's noisy efforts as he stumbled around in the darkness trying to answer it without disturbing her.

She reached out and flicked on the light, just as Ben lifted the receiver. "Hello, Doctor Hemingway speaking."

It was still dark. Sara peered at the clock and groaned, but Ben was now fully awake.

"Right," he said. "OK. I'll tell Sara and I'll be there in ten minutes."

He reached for the clothes he'd laid out on the chair the night before and began to dress quickly. Sara watched him, her head still fuzzy from sleep.

"Who was that?" she asked sleepily.

"It was Jane Phipps, the midwife." He grinned. "Your friend Melissa's in labour!"

"Oh, no! She's won the bet!" Sara exclaimed, patting her large bump wistfully. And she wasn't due for another week!

"Give her my love . . ."

"I will. Now go back to sleep, darling," he said, bending to kiss her quickly on the forehead.

"Some hope," Sara muttered to herself, since there was no comfortable way to lie any more.

She heaved herself out of bed and wandered over to the window. It was dark and damp outside.

Early morning fog hovered around the street lights and as Ben drove off, the mist blurred his red tail lights before finally swallowing them up.

She shivered and reached for her dressing-gown as the cold seeped into her bones.

The dressing-gown was huge and voluminous, but only just fitted around her now that she was in the final weeks of her pregnancy.

In the kitchen, she sat at the table, sipping tea and thinking of Melissa.

She hoped everything was going well. But, of course, she'd have her husband, Neil, there, rubbing her back, mopping her brow and whispering those important words of encouragement and comfort.

"How I envy you, Melissa," she said aloud, tears in her eyes. The baby responded by pushing a fist or a knee hard into Sara's side.

It was reassuring to feel the baby move when it had been unusually still for several hours. Strange how, over the weeks and months, you became used to having something living inside you, moving about . . .

She'd never forget that first movement, no more than a tiny, whispering flutter deep inside.

"I felt it move, Ben!" she'd cried. They'd been in the middle of supper and she'd hurried round the table. "Quick, Ben . . . feel . . ."

He'd laughed and put down his knife and fork.

"Only you can feel it at this stage, Sara," he'd said gently. "I told you it would be any time now, didn't I?" His calm rejection had disappointed her.

Melissa said Neil had been so excited and full of wonder when she'd told him about her baby's first movement. He'd attended all the ante-natal classes with her, too, as did all the other husbands with the exception of Ben, who was always on duty.

Only Sara had no-one . . .

"I can't just drop my clinic," Ben had said when Sara had asked him to go along. "Besides, I'm a doctor, I know what to do!"

So Sara had been the "demonstration model", used by the physiotherapist to show the others what to do.

"Of course, your husband will do this for you at the birth," the physio would say as she massaged Sara's back.

And Sara would think truculently, Will he? Will he even be there? I wonder.

SHE rose from the table and wandered back to the bedroom. The crib stood beside the bed, ready and waiting for its brand-new occupant.

If only Ben would show some enthusiasm. She tried to imagine his excitement at holding his child for the first time, and just couldn't conjure up the picture at all. He was so cool, so calm, about it all.

Over the past few weeks, the baby paraphernalia had grown and grown so that Sara couldn't go anywhere in the house without being reminded of her pregnancy. And each day her anxiety about the birth grew.

Only the day before, in an effort to keep her mind busy, she'd exhausted herself getting the house straight.

Perhaps she shouldn't have. Suddenly Sara stiffened as she felt the strangest sensation . . .

Oh no, the baby must be on the way and Ben wasn't here! She'd always assumed he'd be around when it happened and he'd know what to do.

She mustn't panic. She couldn't — wouldn't — disturb him at the hospital.

Instead, she took a deep breath. Keep calm, she whispered.

Her bag for the hospital had been packed for weeks. Now as she sorted through the baby clothes for the umpteenth time, she was struck by how tiny they were.

How would she ever be able to handle something so small as the wearer?

Before she'd decided what her next move would be, Ben appeared, weary and dark-eyed. Sara, relieved to see him, ran to hug him.

"It's a girl," he announced, grinning. "Louisa. Eight pounds two ounces. Both parents doing fine!"

"Was Neil there?" Sara whispered.

"Held her hand all the way!" he said, smiling. "And Melissa says to get a move on — she wants you to keep her company!"

"I think I —" Sara began.

"Is that coffee?" He crossed to the work-top and poured himself a cup. "I'll take this upstairs. I'm going to freshen up and then I've got a clinic at ten."

"Ben, I —"

"Can it wait, darling? I'm going to have to rush as it is and I hate to keep my patients waiting."

"The baby's coming," she whispered to his retreating back. The bathroom door clicked shut behind him, then opened again.

"Did you just say something?" He peered over the landing rail.

"I said, I think I'm in labour."

"What!" He hurried back downstairs and started firing questions at her; the type of medical questions any doctor would ask his patient.

Not once did he ask how she felt, how she really felt inside.

Not once did he touch her hand or put his arm around her or do anything affectionate to show he was pleased or even concerned.

"I'll call the hospital," he said briskly. "Is everything ready?"

She nodded and he made the call.

When he put the phone down, she touched his arm.

"Ben," she said. "I'm — I'm scared . . ."

"Of course you are, love." He smiled tenderly at her. "But I'll be with you all the time. Stop worrying. It'll be OK. I'll just ring James and get him to do clinic duty for me."

She stood in the hall while he called his colleague.

He knew exactly what he was doing and there was never any question of him panicking. He should have married someone who'd have been as cool and matter-of-fact as himself about such a momentous event, she thought miserably. Not a school teacher, who only had experience of six-year-olds!

She didn't know the first thing about babies — except what they'd taught her at the ante-natal classes, and even then she was terrified about putting what she'd learned into practice.

When she'd voiced her fears to Ben, he'd shaken his head and laughed. "Don't worry. In my experience, it all comes naturally. Within a few days, you'll know instinctively how to handle your own baby. Believe me!"

But Sara was not convinced.

ONCE at the hospital, nothing happened. Sara looked in on her friend, Melissa, and found her sleeping soundly. Then she had a bath, wandered up and down the corridors, or sat in the day-room waiting impatiently for the first twinge.

Nothing.

It wasn't going by the book — it wasn't going at all!

"Don't look so worried," Ben said calmly. If he were any more laid back, Sara thought, he'd be stretched out on the floor fast asleep!

"I am worried," she cried. "Why's nothing happening, Ben?"

"It will." He laughed softly. "Trust me, darling. I know about these things."

"Oh yes, I know you know!" she snapped. "Maybe you know all there is to know about the medical mechanics of things! What you don't seem to know or understand, is what's going on in here!" She tapped her chest.

Ben's smile widened infuriatingly.

"Your heart's lower down than that! Don't worry about letting off steam," he said casually. "That's very normal. Lots of women yell and shout during labour."

"Aaaaargh!" Sara screamed. "I'm going to see if Melissa's awake." And she stormed back into the corridor.

Melissa was indeed awake, sitting up in bed, her baby daughter in her arms, and looking extremely pleased with herself.

"Your turn now, Sara," she said with a laugh. "What's keeping you? If you give birth before midnight, our offspring will share a birthday! We can take turns at throwing the birthday parties!"

"She's beautiful," Sara said softly. "I bet Neil's over the moon."

Melissa beamed. "He's like the proverbial dog with two tails! He was in tears and laughing all at the same time.

"Honestly, though, I'm glad he was there, Sara . . . I don't think I'd have coped half so well without him."

Gently Sara touched Louisa's wispy black hair.

"It won't be long now," Melissa said softly, squeezing Sara's arm. "Is Ben here?"

Sara nodded.

"Good. He'll take care of you. You're lucky being married to a doctor . . . poor Neil didn't know what was happening half the time, despite all the classes and everything.

"But he didn't pass out or go green or anything like that, so I'm not complaining!"

"I just wish it would hurry up and happen," Sara said with a sigh.

Then, leaving Melissa to drool over her precious bundle, she slipped back into the corridor. Ben had seen it all before, many times — that was the trouble. To him, giving birth was nothing out of the ordinary, although she had hoped that the birth of his own child would have been different for him — special. A forlorn hope on her part.

THE sound of Sister's voice boomed down the corridor and it sounded very much as though someone had managed to get on her wrong side.

". . . and I don't care who you are," Sister was saying. "This is my ward and I won't stand for interference of any kind!"

"But things should be moving by now!"

What? Sara stopped in her tracks. That strained, uncertain voice belonged to Ben!

"As it happens, Doctor Hemingway —" Sister's voice was icy "— I've already called in Doctor Stubbs — he'll decide whether we need to start her off or not!"

"Let me see her notes, I . . ."

"May I remind you that you are here in the capacity of expectant father —" she continued firmly "— not as Sara's doctor. And as such, I shall treat you as I would any other potential parent.

"Try to relax and leave it to us. You're too personally involved to think rationally!"

"But she's my wife!" Ben wailed. "I only want what's best for her and our baby! That's all."

Sister gave a wry laugh.

"Oh, yes, it's different when it's your own, isn't it?"

When Sara finally entered the day room, Sister had gone and Ben was standing staring out of the window.

He grinned. "Ah, there you are. Any pains yet?"

She shook her head and stared at him, trying to work out what he was thinking.

"Not to worry," he said brightly. "Sister's getting Doctor Stubbs to come in. He may decide to help things along a little, nothing to worry about, darling."

"You mean he's going to induce me?"

"Maybe . . . we'll just have to wait and see."

He sounded so glib now, so casual. He was doing it, she realised now, so as not to frighten her, but the strange thing was, she was no longer scared.

At some stage, a sense of peace had settled about her and she felt relaxed.

"Are you frightened?" she said at last.

Ben looked stunned.

"Me?" He laughed. "Of course not! There's nothing to be frightened of."

"Of course there isn't," she said reassuringly. "Everything's going to be fine!"

They stared at each other then, puzzled. Somehow their roles had changed. He was the anxious one, while she was calm and in control.

He looked shattered.

His hair stuck up in spikes and there was dark stubble on his chin. He looked every inch a typical, anxious, expectant father.

B Y tea-time, with a little assistance, labour was well under way. Ben mopped Sara's face, held her hand too tightly and kept issuing orders to the midwife — which she studiously ignored.

"Doctor Hemingway!" the midwife snapped at last. "Everything is progressing normally! Your wife is coping perfectly well and if you can't do the same, I shall have to ask you to leave the labour suite!"

Ben grinned sheepishly at Sara and shrugged and she felt a surge of love for him even through a painful contraction.

"Remember your breathing, darling," Ben whispered anxiously, and she heard his voice through the haze. It wasn't an instruction from a doctor, but a concerned plea from a worried husband.

And then at last: "Here it comes!" the midwife announced triumphantly and Ben almost toppled his chair in his haste to glimpse the first sight of his baby. His face was alight with joy and wonder.

He turned back to Sara and clasped her hand lovingly as another contraction brought their baby closer into the world.

The birth was over quickly after that and their little son was placed in Sara's arms. Immediately he stopped bawling and regarded her with knowing slate-blue eyes.

Sara looked up at Ben. Tears of happiness welled up in his eyes.

"Here, you hold him." She passed the baby to him and he took his baby son from her carefully.

"He . . . he's beautiful," he said softly. "I've delivered dozens of babies in my time, Sara . . . and I'm not just saying this because he's ours, but he's the most beautiful baby I've ever seen . . ."

His voice wobbled and Sara smiled.

The baby's face crumpled and he began to scream. Ben's face crumpled, too, and this man who'd held dozens of new-born babies suddenly looked worried and unsure of himself.

"Don't worry, darling," Sara said calmly, taking the baby from him. "He just wants his mum!"

"Ah," Ben looked relieved. "Well, there you are!" His confidence was coming back. "Didn't I tell you there was nothing to worry about?"

"Yes," Sara agreed. "Yes, you did and you were right."

She'd been silly to fear the arrival of this child, because the minute he'd been placed in her arms, it had felt right.

But most of all, she'd done Ben a terrible injustice in thinking he didn't care, when it was obvious now that he did.

"I love you," she said vehemently, putting her arms round his neck.

"And I love you, too," he said, kissing her tenderly. "Both of you. So very much." ■

Nothing Steve said or did could
convince her that David
wasn't coming back.

"I'LL WAIT FOR YOU..."

by Isobel Stewart

THROUGH all the long months, Lynn held on to the absolute certainty that David would come back to her. "This isn't real," she told him, and despite the shock, she had been proud of the steadiness of her voice.

"You're infatuated with her. She's young, she's exciting — it's a mid-life crisis, that's all. You'll get over it. I'll wait until you do."

Afterwards, she wondered — was it pity in his eyes, as he shook his head?

"No, Lynn." His voice, too, was steady. "It isn't any of these things. I'm deeply sorry that I'm doing this to you and the children.

"Believe me, I have tried. But I love Alison and I want a divorce so that we can be married."

You don't love her, she had thought with certainty. You love me. You've lost sight of that for the moment, but you'll come to your senses, and you'll know. And I will wait.

That night, he left her. And the waiting began.

She couldn't remember when she stopped telling people it would only be temporary. Perhaps it was when the divorce went through, or when David married Alison. Perhaps it was when she began to notice that people looked away, embarrassed, awkward, when she said it.

But her own certainty was still there, even when she heard that David and Alison were expecting their first child.

When she heard that the baby was a girl, for a moment she experienced a dreadful longing. Dearly as I love my two boys I always wanted a little girl, she thought painfully. And now she has David's daughter.

That night, alone in her bedroom, the room that had been David's and hers for so many years, she cried.

But at last she dried her tears, and lifted her chin. At least I have his sons, she told herself. And he will come back to us when this is all over, when he comes to his senses.

Everyone said how reasonable Lynn was being about it all. How civilised. David himself said it, awkwardly, more than once, when he was collecting the boys.

And it was true. Lynn was making a conscious effort not to turn the boys against their father.

In the early days, when they had come home from a visit, and Simon had said eagerly, "She's nice, Mum, Alison is," Gary had frowned a warning at him, but Lynn had just smiled.

"Of course she is," she had agreed, brightly. "Your father wouldn't choose anyone who wasn't nice, would he?" There was no bitterness in her voice.

Yes, she thought, I could have influenced the boys, turned them against their father. I could have made them feel torn between us, disloyal to me when they see him. But if I did, that would only make things hard for us all, when he finally comes back.

She had never said anything to the boys about her feeling that David would return. It was like a secret lifeline, so secret that no-one else must know about it.

Which was why she was so taken aback when Steve realised . . .

STEVE had been part of their lives — hers and David's — for years. He lived two houses away and was a teacher at the local High School. In his spare time he worked as stage manager for the local Dramatic Society.

Sometimes he dated one of the other teachers, or one of the girls from the Dramatic Society, but somehow nothing ever came of it.

"It's strange really," Lynn used to say to David. "He seems too nice not to be married." Strange or not, it was something, Lynn had to admit, that she was quite glad of now she was on her own.

Steve was always there to help out with a flat tyre, with a blocked drain, with the boys' homework.

From time to time he came round to have a meal with them, and sometimes he suggested that they should all go for a picnic.

Both Gary and Simon were as fond of him as Lynn was herself, and she wondered what they would have done without him.

It was after a day at the funfair that everything changed.

They'd all been pleasantly tired, and both the boys were flushed with excitement. Lynn made risotto and the boys had been allowed to stay up and watch TV.

Later, after the boys were in bed, Steve unexpectedly reached over and took both her hands in his.

"Let's go and sit down," he said, and there was something different, something strange, in his voice. "I'll help you with the dishes after, but first I want to talk to you, Lynn."

Unresisting, she allowed him to lead her to the couch and sat looking at him, waiting for him to speak.

"You're not making this easy for me," Steve said at last. He smiled but his grey eyes were clouded. "Somehow, I didn't think I'd ever have to put it into words.

"I thought I'd given you long enough to work it out for yourself, but I can't wait any longer."

He took a deep breath. "You must know how I feel about you, Lynn."

"I don't know what the boys and I would do without you, without your friendship," she said quickly.

He shook his head.

"Not just friendship, my dear. It's grown beyond that. I love you, Lynn. I've loved you for a long time."

Then his arms were around her, and his lips on hers. And for a treacherous moment her arms went round him, too, and she moved closer to him.

But only for a moment. Then she drew back out of his arms.

"No, Steve, it wouldn't be right," she said, and her own voice was unsteady.

"Wouldn't be right?" he repeated, taken aback, and then — slowly — understanding dawned in his eyes.

"You still think David will come back to you," he said flatly. It wasn't a question.

She looked away, but not quickly enough, because she saw that now there was pity in his eyes.

"Lynn, my dear," he said, and his voice was gentle. "You and David have been divorced for two years. He has Alison, he has a child with her. You can't think he'll come back to you."

She repeated the old familiar words.

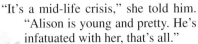

"It's a mid-life crisis," she told him. "Alison is young and pretty. He's infatuated with her, that's all."

Once again, he took her hands in his, and she didn't draw away.

"You might have thought that at first, but surely you can't think that now? He and Alison are married, they have a baby. You must see that if it was just infatuation, it would have been over by now?"

She shook her head. "I can wait," she said.

Steve was silent for a long time.

"So can I," he said at last and when he left, he kissed her cheek, as he always had done, as a friend.

IN the days and weeks after that, Lynn might almost have believed that the strange, disturbing conversation had never taken place.

Steve went on helping the boys with their homework, he took her out for a meal, or to a film, when Gary and Simon spent the weekend with David, he changed the tyre on her car for her, he mended the chain of Gary's bicycle.

But sometimes, Lynn would look up and find his eyes resting on her, steady, patient. And other times, when his hand brushed against hers accidentally, in the car, in the cinema, she would find herself remembering his lips on hers, remembering her own involuntary response to him.

Once, he happened to be at the house when David came to collect the boys.

The two men greeted each other a little awkwardly, for as Lynn knew, they had met only briefly since David moved out.

She listened as they talked about work, and for a moment Steve's eyes met hers. Unaccountably she found her cheeks warm.

"How is the baby, David?" she asked brightly.

"Fine, thank you," David replied. He smiled but the smile didn't reach his eyes. "Well, mostly she's fine. A little colicky, but you know what babies are."

Oh yes, I know what babies are, Lynn thought. I remember when our two were babies. Do you remember that too, David?

Do you look at Alison, do you look at this baby, and do you wonder what you are doing there, with them, instead of being here with me, with your sons?

Are you beginning to realise that you were wrong, are you beginning to see that this is where you should be, where you want to be?

The boys came downstairs then, carrying towels and swimming trunks.

"Are we still going to the swimming-pool, Dad?" Simon asked eagerly.

David nodded. "We'll go for an hour on the way home," he said. "I want to se that diving you've both been practising."

Home.

It was disturbing, hearing him say the word so easily, so casually. She pushed the feeling away. What else would he say, after all, to describe the place he and Alison lived in?

★ ★ ★ ★

That night she went with Steve to the rehearsal of the play the Dramatic Society were putting on.

Lynn knew some of the other people, and although Steve, as stage manager, was busy most of the time, she rather enjoyed watching the play begin to take shape.

"I can see why you enjoy the Dramatic Society," she said to Steve as they walked home. "It's fun."

"How about joining?" His voice was casual. "You don't have to take a part — you could be my assistant, at least at first."

"Oh, no, I couldn't do that," she said quickly. "I — I couldn't leave the boys."

His grey eyes were steady, stopping her from looking away.

"You know you'd only be five minutes away, in the church hall," he pointed out. "And babysitters aren't in short supply . . .

"You have to begin to make a life for yourself. You can't sit around waiting for David to come back to you . . . it just isn't going to happen."

She didn't say anything. He pushed her garden gate open, and they walked up the path.

At the door he took her key from her and unlocked the front door. Usually he came in with her because he knew she was nervous about going into the empty and silent house. But now he stood looking down at her, unsmiling.

"Are you coming in for coffee, Steve?" she asked at last.

"No thanks." His voice was tight, controlled. "I'm finding this waiting game harder than I thought, Lynn. Sorry, I think I'd better go."

Dismayed, she stood at the door as he strode down the path, and along the road to his own house.

THE house had never before seemed so empty, so lonely. She missed the boys, of course, but somehow this loneliness was different — as though she'd brought it on herself.

The sudden ring of the telephone startled her. She hurried across the hall. Was it Steve?

It was David.

"Sorry, Lynn, I know it's late," he said, "but Gary forgot to bring his school project, and I promised I'd give him a hand with it tomorrow. All right if I come over now and pick it up?"

She said that was all right, and replaced the receiver, confused by that moment of disappointment when she'd realised it wasn't Steve.

That's just because we've been friends so long, she told herself. I hate for us to part the way we did.

It wasn't long before she heard the once-familiar sound of David's car in the drive, and it was only when she opened the door that she realised that this was the first time since he'd left her that they had been alone together.

The boys had always been there with them, before this. She wondered if he had realised it too, as she handed David Gary's project.

"Thanks, Lynn," he said. "Sorry to bother you so late, but Gary was upset when he realised he'd forgotten it. I phoned earlier, but you were out."

"I was at a rehearsal of the play with Steve," she said, annoyed with herself for the warm tide of colour she felt in her cheeks.

"I'm glad you did that," he said unexpectedly. "You need to get out more."

This was dangerous ground, and she could see that he realised that as soon as he had said it.

"I was just going to have coffee," she said. "Would you like some?"

He shook his head. "No, thanks, I must get back. I promised Alison I'd fix a dripping tap in the bathroom for her.

"She hears it when she's up at night feeding Mandy, and it's driving her nuts. I only got the washer today, but I must get back and fix it."

When he had gone, she went

slowly into the kitchen but she didn't switch on the kettle. Instead, she stood at the sink, looking at her own taps, and thinking of David going back to fix a dripping tap for Alison.

And suddenly, completely, his new marriage was real. Real, and lasting.

She imagined Alison — not glamorous, but tired — her blonde hair rumpled, up at night to feed the baby. And not just the baby but Mandy, David's daughter. David's daughter. David's child, just as much as Gary and Simon were his children.

She imagined Alison in a comfortable old dressing-gown, as she herself used to be all those years ago when the boys were babies and she got up to feed them.

And she thought of a dripping tap, a tap that Alison knew David would fix for her . . .

Lynn sat down at the kitchen table. David would go on mending dripping taps for Alison, building new memories, in this new marriage. But theirs, she knew at last, was over.

She didn't know that she was crying until she felt a tear fall from her cheek to her hand. But somehow there was healing and acceptance in these tears, and she let herself weep.

When she heard the knock at the door, she knew it was Steve.

"I should have checked the house for you," he said, his voice still abrupt. "I'm sorry, Lynn, I know you don't like coming in on your own. I'll —"

He stopped, and looked at her.

"You've been crying." Gently, with one finger, he traced the tearstains on her cheeks.

"Oh, Lynn, love," he said, not quite steadily. "I didn't mean to make you cry."

"You didn't make me cry," she told him. "David was here, but he's gone now."

He looked at her, his eyes holding hers, questioning, for a long time. And then, satisfied, he nodded.

Some day, she would tell him everything, but she could see that for now, she didn't have to say any more. He understood . . .

"I'll go now," he said, quietly. "Now that I know you're . . . all right."

She went with him to the door. For a moment, he held her close to him. It was what she needed at the moment, nothing more. Not yet.

"I'll see you tomorrow," he said.

At the gate, he turned and waved.

"See you tomorrow," she repeated, and she could see that he heard the promise and the assurance in the word.

Tomorrow . . . ■

The Reluctant Traveller

by Joyce Stranger

Tired and abandoned, the little collie had to find shelter from the storm and comfort from the fear that haunted her . . .

SHE was alone. She was hungry. She was unwanted. She was a beautiful little collie with a sad face and a thick brown and white coat. The white fur on her chest marked her with distinction.

She stared across the fields at dark, towering trees and a sky marked with gathering clouds. All this was new and terrifying territory.

They had taken her out in the car two days before. Excitement mastered her, for this was a well-loved routine, and, for weeks, it had been forgotten.

In happier days they always took her for a race on the beach and a long run, and they all came home tired and smelling of sea-salt. Then she would lie by the fire in the evening and listen to the cadence of the voices.

Once they had been happy voices and they had spoken to her gently. Then they changed and were angry, loud, and abusive. She, too, was shouted at, and found herself too often in the way.

The words "out of work" were said more and more often and seemed to make the man and woman even more angry.

She tried to make herself small, always to do as she was told, but sometimes the man gave her one order and the woman another, and then she was confused.

She was punished, but never understood why.

That day they had not driven to the beach. Instead, they drove miles from home, and tied her by a rope to a post.

She was used to that, though. They would take food from the car and sit and eat and laugh and talk, and then they would free her, and she would run and play.

But that did not happen this time — something was different. Cars sped past her and she was afraid.

She crouched against the ground, and then looked up in disbelief as the man and woman drove away, leaving her behind.

She cried to them, telling them that they had forgotten her. Her forlorn howls followed them as they accelerated away, and finally, unbelievably, the blur in the distance was gone and the road was empty.

Nobody came . . .

She chewed the rope, desperate, and, when she was free, galloped along the hard tarmac beside the cars, trying desperately to find the only people she had known in her short life. She didn't understand why they had gone — or that they were never coming back.

IT was the young lads on their motor-bikes who saw her first. They had spent the day racing along muddy trails in the woods, and their blood was up.

When the leading biker saw the startled collie, he gave an excited whoop, revved his engine and raced across the damp ground towards her. Without stopping to think, the others followed.

Frightened, she raced up the bank, away from the road, and into the woods. Here she was able to dart and dodge, but the relentless roar followed her, and soon there came searching lights, loud voices and the sharp smell of petrol.

Pounding heart thudding in her chest; tearing breath gasping from her lungs; fear dominating every thought.

Dusk was sighing into darkness. The lights and voices no longer pursued her, but she carried on running anyway — too scared to stop.

There was a wind in her face, a spiteful, chilling wind, easing the trees that rustled eerily above her. She was not used to darkness and to the night-time ways.

She had been afraid of doing wrong at home, but this lonely fear of the unknown was new to her.

Her life till now had been calm, untouched by terror. The only enemies she had known were those nagging, shrill voices, but now her world had been turned upside down.

There were enemies behind every bush; enemies behind every tree; enemies waiting for her at every turn.

She was nervous and uncertain in the woods. She was used to open spaces and wide beaches. She loved the tang in the air at the seaside and the long strands of weed that she took and raced with and dropped. Life had been fun, once, she remembered.

Here the ground smelled wet and musty and the overhanging trees shook and dropped twigs on her. The wind swirled and roared, and unseen fingers flew through her brown and white coat.

Still she dodged and darted, her ears flat to her head, her eyes wide and frightened; scared, tired, alone.

When she reached the edge of the wood, she stopped. She could go back into the trees or take the path that led downwards to the houses.

She did not know if people were to be trusted ever again. People had abandoned her. There had been noisy people behind her, intent on some game that she did not understand.

Tree branches rustled in the wind and rain began to fall in a steady, miserable drizzle. Her mind was made up.

Where there were houses, there might be shelter. She trotted warily down towards the village.

The path twisted down the side of the hill, and lingered beside the stream. Here the trees grew close to the water, and the banks were sodden with overspill. Cruel brambles caught at her, tearing at her legs.

The ghost of a moon soared up the sky, silvering the woods, and still she ran on. Away from the woods, away from the terrifying chase and away from the place where the people she loved and trusted had left her to her fate.

Pausing for breath, she took in air in great gulps that filled her lungs and dizzied her head.

Her body ached for rest and her mind yelled for help, but she knew there would be none.

THERE was a bite in the night air, and, harsh on the cool breeze, she caught the sharp tang of a coal fire, as she cautiously skirted the village.

She was nearing the edge of the garden of the last house, an outlying cottage, on its own, smoke pluming from the chimney.

There was the smell of cooking food on the air, and she looked longingly at the curtained windows, cracks of light spilling over the ground.

Was there safety there? Or was there more to fear?

A car swished past, orange in the street lamps, and she turned into a narrow lane, instinctively seeking quieter streets — wary of people.

The alley twisted.

A huge tawny cat hissed and spat and ran. She trotted on, faster now, the cobbles under her feet easier to run on than the muddy woodland path.

The ghost moon brightened and shone on the alleyway. It shone on a gateway in a high wall — on a gate that stood ajar.

She slipped through it into a small, well-tended garden.

The curtained light of a window cast faint shadows across the yard, and a door stood open as an old woman went out to her dustbin.

There was no time to think. She was close to exhaustion; sanctuary was imperative.

The old woman did not see the collie as the animal slunk behind her and into the bright kitchen. But when the woman came back indoors and caught sight of the intruder, she gave a startled gasp.

The dog flinched and the woman bent down to her stiffly, her voice comforting.

"All right, my pretty, I won't harm you," she said, and held out her hand for the collie to sniff, before opening the door from the kitchen into the sitting-room.

Sensing no danger, the exhausted animal followed the old lady into a gently-lit room with curtains drawn and a log fire crackling cheerily in the grate.

The old woman picked up her knitting and watched the flames flicker.

The collie crept to her, and put her head on the bony knee.

"I lost my Laddie three weeks ago," the old woman told her. "Fifteen years we had together and I missed his company so much but couldn't afford to buy another dog."

The voice was soft and kind. The collie wagged a tentative tail.

"He went sudden, did my Laddie," she continued. "I found him asleep for ever in his basket one morning last month."

Her eyes misted over and she swallowed, then, with a determined shake of her head, she stood up. "There's an empty basket and bowl and plenty of food in the cupboard for you, my pretty one," she said. "I haven't been able to bring myself to throw them out."

The collie watched the old lady as she opened a tin of dog food and put it in a yellow bowl on the floor. She was not yet sure of her welcome, and crouched, eyes pleading.

The old woman brought the bowl and set it in front of her. Gentle hands touched the fur on the little bitch's neck.

"No collar; and by the look of those pads of yours you've come a long way. Someone dumped you, I'd guess. I'll ask around, but I think you're my dog now, my pretty, and most welcome you are, too." Her face brightened as a thought struck her. "Maybe my Laddie showed you the way to come . . ."

Nobody claimed her.

As the years went by, the old lady often sat under the apple tree in her garden, the collie, whom she named Belle, stretched out beside her.

Her sons were told of the night that the little stray flew to her for sanctuary, and gained a home. They laughed gently at their mother's belief that this was meant to happen.

Belle often sat by the garden wall and stared out over the woods. Far away and long ago she had had another life, but that was forgotten now.

Soon, the village looked for them on their daily excursions; the old woman walking proudly, the little collie with the white fur on her chest trotting happily at her heels — never once leaving her side. ∎

*She longed to
share it...
but some
things are
better kept
to oneself...*

Secret From The Past

*by Teresa
Ashby*

A^S I approached the common I saw rabbits enjoying the early morning
sunshine stop in their tracks and sit up, ears cocked, listening intently.

Shane saw the rabbits too and took off, feathery legs pounding across the
sun-streaked grass, his joyful bark scattering them in all directions.

You'd think he'd have got the hang of chasing rabbits by now, but he
romps round in circles and ends up standing in the middle of an empty field,
a puzzled expression in his gentle, dark eyes, while the rabbits hide in their
burrows.

It was lovely out this morning, a really beautiful spring morning with the sun streaming through the fresh green leaves, bathing everything in its warm light. But I didn't want to stay out long because today it's your birthday.

Not just any birthday, but a very special one. You're 21 today.

Shane sits by his water bowl watching as I move about the empty kitchen. I've slanted the blinds so that the sun will pour in and warm me, because I'm feeling very cold all of a sudden.

As always, on your birthday it is another day that comes to mind and, perhaps because today is so special, it is more vivid in my memory than usual.

In a strange way, it is like looking back at someone else's life, as though none of it really happened to me at all. Yet how well I remember the despair . . .

It's so deep inside me but I can still feel an ache, even though so many years have passed. There is so much I wish I could say to you, but I can't, so I say it to myself and pretend you're here listening to me . . .

I coped with it all pretty well, I suppose. Leaving school when my pregnancy began to show, going through the agony of telling my parents, knowing that people were pointing at me and talking.

I don't recall being frightened of giving birth to you. Being young, I suppose I just accepted what was happening to me, to my body, even taking time to wonder at the changes occurring.

Like the first time I felt you move inside me. I felt like rushing outside and shouting it out for everyone to hear. My baby moved! Until then, you weren't real.

Then, something strange happened. I began to talk to you, touching my swollen abdomen as though I could reach you somehow. I didn't know whether you were a girl or a boy, but somehow that didn't matter. I loved you.

My parents were very supportive. We kept having "family conferences" as my mum called them, when we would all sit around the dining-table, drinking coffee and discussing your future — and mine.

With me being the eldest of four, it was decided that it would be impossible and unfair to expect my parents to take care of you. Besides, we were a bit cramped in the house as it was with such a large family.

There were hundreds of couples desperate for a baby of their own, my mum said. It would be best for everyone if you went to one of them.

Even then, before you were born, while you were still a part of me, I felt a sense of loss at these words, knowing that I would give you life, then have to let you go.

My school was very understanding and I continued my education at home. After you were born, I would go back and resume full-time education.

Where did your father . . . Oh, it's still so hard to believe that that young, thin boy was your father! Where did he fit in? The truth was, he didn't. I loved Martin, but somehow that love fizzled out during my pregnancy and he started going out with someone else. I wasn't heartbroken or hurt.

After all, I still had you.

THEY told me to try not to think of you as a person with a separate identity. It would be easier to let you go then. And I had a bright future ahead of me without you. An exciting career after art college as a graphic designer.

It was all planned. Getting pregnant was merely a hiccup in the trim line of events.

They said it was because I was young and fit that giving birth was so easy. I don't remember much pain at all, just the joy of holding you in my arms afterwards and gazing down at your perfect little face and feeling a surge of love flood through me.

They had wanted to take you from me right away, but I managed to wheedle and manipulate my way into keeping you for six weeks. I used to buy you little dresses and lacy matinee jackets and dress you up like a little doll.

My parents said I was wasting my money, but I knew I didn't have you for long and I wanted to spoil you. They were becoming impatient. Understandably I suppose. They had come to think of broken nights and nappies drying over the fireguard as things of the past.

Of course, there wasn't a pram for me to push you around in and your bed was a drawer from my dressing table. My mum had got rid of all her baby stuff after my youngest brother was born.

There was an agreed time, on an agreed day, for me to take you to the office of the social worker who was in charge of "my case". It would be easier for me to say goodbye to you in the cold, impersonal surroundings there than in the warmth of my home.

My parents, naturally, wanted to come with me, but I had to do it alone. I can see myself, if I close my eyes, hurrying along the High Street with you clutched tightly in my arms, two bottles of expressed milk tucked safely in my shoulder bag. The milk was probably the best thing to give you, yet it seemed such a pathetic parting gift.

I remember I wore a mini-skirt and pale pink tights with little diamond patterns down the sides. My long hair hung loose from a centre parting, caught back at each side with a slide.

You were all wrapped up in a soft, white shawl, so that only your sweet little face was on show. Wide awake, you stared up at me as I hurried along.

We had to wait in a little room with abstract paintings on the walls and a ghastly orange carpet on the floor. There were matching orange curtains at the windows, but they'd faded in the wash and shrunk, too.

I talked to you while we waited. Tried to explain, but I suppose I wasn't trying to make sense of it for you, but for myself.

It's for the best. I've got my future to think of — and, more importantly, your future.

A nice couple with a nice house and a nice garden would take you home and make you theirs. You'd grow up to be a nice child and when you were old enough, maybe, somehow, you'd find me and we'd be like strangers.

You'd always wonder why I'd given you away and perhaps, somewhere in your heart, you'd resent me for it.

She was sorry to keep me waiting, the social worker with the long brown hair and calf-length kaftan. She wore strings of chunky brown beads around her neck and thick, ethnic bracelets. Her fingers were smothered with huge, silver rings, but her smile was warm.

For the first time since I first discovered I was pregnant, I was filled again with despair and I couldn't hold back the tears as they flooded down my cheeks and dripped on to your lacy shawl.

Gently she said, why don't you write her a letter — something for her to treasure when she's older? And then she went away and fetched me some paper.

Still holding you close, I tried to explain to you — or to the person you would be one day in the far distant future — why I had to part with you.

Numbly I listed my reasons for giving you up and one phrase seemed to keep repeating itself.

For the best. The best for you, the best for me, the best for the social worker who could write me off her books as a satisfactory case, happily concluded.

Best for the boy who was your father and was afraid now even to speak to me and best for the teachers who had all been shocked and upset by my fall from grace.

When I'd finished, she came back and asked if she could read it. I shrugged and handed it to her. I'll never forget the way she read it, then crumpled it in her fist and threw it into the wastepaper basket in the corner.

It was one of those baskets that look a bit like a sheaf of wheat. It's funny how details like that stick with you. The wicker bin, the orange curtains, the angry look in the dark eyes of the social worker.

SHANE rubs his wet nose against my leg and I realise that the kitchen is filling with steam. The automatic turn-off on the kettle doesn't always work and I have to rush across to switch it off.

The teapot's filled and snuggling under a tea-cosy which has a fat cat appliquéd on to it. I have a few seconds to reflect on the peace and quiet of a spring Sunday morning when there is a noise above my head. The scampering of little feet upstairs. That's Gavin awake.

Now there's another voice up there. That's Jamie. He's nine and he'll be telling his little brother to be quiet.

A deep, rumbling voice joins in. That's Keith, my husband. He'll be trying to keep the peace between our sons.

Quickly, I set cups out and pour milk into two and tea into the rest, then I carry the tray carefully to the stairs. Keith sees me coming and takes the tray.

He puts it on the little table on the landing, while I hurry into our bedroom and rummage through my wardrobe.

"Ready?" Keith says and I nod.

The boys have already guzzled their drinks and their empty cups are on the floor. Now there's only one cup left on the tray and I put the cards which arrived yesterday beside it. Then Keith knocks on the door and carries it in.

I look at you, lying there sound asleep, and my heart swells with love, just as it did all those years ago. You're still just as beautiful.

"Happy birthday!" The boys yell in unison and you sit right up and hold out your arms so that they run to you and give you a huge birthday hug.

Like a little child, you don't know whether to grab your tea or your cards first.

Looking at you so happy and so loved by your family brings the tears to my eyes.

I owe so very much to that social worker who threw my letter in the bin and told me to take you home and love you!

She said she'd do all she could to help me — and she did. She helped me find a little flat and a good child-minder to take care of you while I went to work to support us.

It wasn't easy, sometimes it was a downright nightmare, but I never, not once, regretted keeping you.

I didn't regret not going to art college, nor look with sadness upon my career . . . In the end I didn't lose out on my career.

Just yesterday, I was told that some illustrations I'd done had been accepted by a publisher.

"Happy birthday, darling," I say softly, as I bend down to kiss you.

As I said, there is so much I wish I could tell you, but some things, perhaps, are best left unsaid.

Maybe one day, I will tell you the story of how I came so close to giving you away, but the moment, it's a secret which belongs to me alone. ■

Haunted by her memories, she waited for her loved one to return from the sea...

In Silent Vigil

by Teresa Ashby

M ARION REID was washing up
when she heard the blast of the
distress signal tearing through
the silent sky. She stopped, her hands
submerged in the bubbles, and listened
for the swish of the second flare as it
soared upwards before exploding high
above the village.

For a few painful seconds, the world
seemed to stop turning as she looked
towards the table. John had been reading

the newspaper and as she watched, he got to his feet. Everything was happening so slowly. John reaching for his jacket, the newspaper spread across the table, its pages all over the place.

He came over to her, placed his big hands on her shoulders and kissed her forehead.

"I'll be back," he said softly. "Don't worry."

She tried to speak, but her throat had closed and even as the door slammed shut behind him, her hands were still in the washing-up water, her face still wearing its mask of shock.

Everything so normal, so agonisingly real, yet here she was, suspended in unreality, unable to move.

Although the evening sun beamed across the distant fields, glowing warmly against the white walls of the cottage, Marion knew that the view from the other side of the cottage, out to sea, told a different story.

In a daze, she moved through the cottage to the front.

From her bedroom window, the sea was the landscape, the forbidding, treacherous sea with its white plumes and deadly currents, dark beneath a leaden grey sky.

The lifeboat suddenly bounced into view, skimming across the waves, so small, no more than an orange and black dot. It was called The Andrew Harrison, named after its last skipper, the man who had died ten years ago on the boat's predecessor.

She'd been there at the new boat's launch. A young, trembling widow, her face colourless, her eyes as dark as a winter sea. Standing proudly, dressed in clothes chosen by a close friend, her nine-year-old son at her side, Marion had presented a brave face to the world.

Behind that brave face, Marion had felt crushed, broken, there only for the sake of her son. He was so proud of his hero father, already tall and unashamed of the tears that filled his eyes but never spilled on to his cheeks.

Eventually, she had come to terms with the loss and the pain, although she could never hear the maroon signal without thinking of Andrew and remembering . . .

As she stood now, at the window, the sea a blur behind the memories, a figure appeared outside. It was a weather-beaten face, framed by a headscarf.

A few wisps of pepper-coloured hair had sprung from beneath the scarf and were being whipped and blown by the wind.

"Marion!"

Jerked out of the past and into the present, she realised that The Andrew Harrison had disappeared from view and she was staring instead into the face of Betty Thornton, the cox's wife.

"I'm going down . . . are you coming?" Betty called above the wind.

"I'll get my coat," Marion called back. "Be with you in a minute."

The two women battled against the wind down to the little harbour. Once there, they stood braced against the rails, rain and salt spray spattering their faces.

"Seems there was a trawler in trouble," Betty said carefully. "About two miles out . . . It's John's first time, isn't it?"

Her face stiff with cold and salt, Marion nodded silently.

"He'll be all right!" Betty squeezed her arm, but Marion wouldn't believe it until she saw him standing in front of her.

"I didn't even say goodbye," she muttered. "He heard the maroon and went, just like that."

"Stop talking as if he isn't coming back!" Betty cried. "Oh, Marion, it's ten years since Skip was killed. We haven't lost a single man since then . . ."

TEN long years . . . "I couldn't bear it, if he . . ." Marion whispered to herself. Betty's acute hearing picked up Marion's words.

"John will be all right," Betty said firmly. "He can look after himself . . . He's not a fool —"

"Neither was Andrew!" Marion retorted sharply, then, overcome with remorse, she turned and faced the older woman. "Oh, Betty, I'm sorry. I didn't mean . . ."

"I know, love." Betty's face broke into a smile. "But you're not alone, look . . ."

She turned and held out her hand. For the first time, Marion saw the others. Women she didn't even know stood with their backs against the rail, their faces grey and lined with worry.

They were the wives and the mothers of the trawlermen. They were the ones who had to live with the fear every day.

Before the sea took Andrew, Marion had taken it for granted that he'd come home. He'd always kiss her and she'd smell the sea on him and his face would be glowing with the knowledge of a job well done. Only rarely he came home sad . . . only rarely.

"I hate it," she said vehemently. "I hate the sea so much."

Betty smiled. "Well, you didn't when you were younger. I remember when you were a little girl, you were hardly out of the water and when it was too cold to swim, you'd be off fishing with the boys!"

Marion smiled despite herself. How could she have forgotten that?

"Without the sea, this village would have died long ago, Marion. I know it's taken life in the past, but it's given us life, too. You shouldn't dwell in the past too much, love.

"When you married again, you should have left the past behind . . . It isn't fair on either of you."

Marion looked away. Betty was right, she had to start looking to the future, but how could she when every time the maroon beckoned, John would race off?

At the time of Andrew's death, remarriage had been unthinkable, but, amazingly, she had fallen in love again and four years ago had taken again those vows to love and to cherish. And new life grew again inside her as the cycle began again and the world turned.

The wait went on, in silence now. The wintry sun finally slipped away and the moon took over, battling to shine through scudding clouds.

There were no stars to be seen.

More people came to stand at the quayside and wait. As the villagers arrived home from work and school, they came to stand in silent vigil.
No-one asked what was going on, they knew instinctively.

Then the steady thrum of a helicopter came up from behind and they all turned to look as the big yellow air-sea rescue machine passed overhead.

Marion tried to quell a sudden surge of fear. Some of the children waved and to their delight, the winchman took time to wave back as they passed.

This had happened the night Andrew had died. The lifeboat had overturned in the heavy seas and hurricane force winds . . .

"It doesn't mean anything," Betty said, reading Marion's thoughts. "The air-sea rescue often comes to help out. It could be they've an injured man who'll need to be winched to safety."

As ambulances arrived and lined up on the quayside, Marion shuddered.

"Marion . . . ?" She heard her name and turned to see Alan, weaving his way through the people. At least he was still here, at least the sea would never steal him.

"John's out on the boat," she said. "They've been gone for ages."

"It'll be all right," he said quietly. He'd said that the night Andrew was killed as he tried to comfort her. He put his arm around her and held her close. She didn't know how she'd have got through the last ten years without him.

"You're cold," he said, concerned, but she didn't feel cold, she didn't feel anything except scared.

IT wasn't long before the helicopter came back. This time there was no waving winchman.

"They'll be taking someone to hospital," Alan surmised. "Look, look . . . !"

Everyone seemed to spot it at the same time. The lights of the lifeboat as she swept through the darkness towards them. They were all craning their necks now, every one of them hoping for the sight of a loved one.

"Will you be all right?" Alan spoke to Marion.

"I'll stay with her," Betty offered. "Off you go."

Alan hurried on down to the pier where The Andrew Harrison would dock. Marion, through all the worry, felt a thrill of pride.

The rescued trawlermen were off first, wrapped in blankets and silver foil. They looked shocked and shaken, but glad to be alive.

Marion, up by the rails, scanned the darkness, then a shout went up from below.

"John!" she cried.

"There you are!" Betty smiled. "What did I tell you? You don't think my Bob would let anything happen to him, do you?"

"Oh, Betty . . ." Eyes filled with tears of relief, Marion joined the other women as they welcomed their men home.

She found John, and hugged him to her in relief.

"You should be proud of him," a woman said as she passed. "If it wasn't for people like him . . ."

The woman's voice broke on a sob and she moved off with her husband towards an ambulance.

"I am proud of you, John, so very proud. I don't want you ever to doubt that."

"That lad of yours did well." Bob, the cox, patted her on the back.

As if by magic, Alan appeared beside them again. He was grinning all over his face.

"I'm off to the hospital now," he said. "The casualty was a man with a fractured leg — nothing too serious. Will you be all right?"

Marion nodded.

"Get him home, into a hot bath and give him something hot to drink," Alan went on. "How do you feel, John?"

"Good," John laughed. "I feel good, but . . ."

As he looked at Marion, she saw the shadow in his eyes and nodded her understanding. Andrew had always come home from rescues feeling good; yet he'd said that somehow, he'd felt pulled up by the experience, made more aware of the awesome power of the sea and the vulnerability of man.

LATER, at home, John sat beside the fire, his face rosy in the glow of the burning coals.

"You shouldn't have stood all that time in your condition!" he grinned. "But thanks. Were you very worried?"

128